Community Studies

Bloomsbury Research Methods
Edited by Graham Crow and Mark Elliot

The Bloomsbury Research Methods series provides authoritative introductions to a range of research methods which are at the forefront of developments in a range of disciplines.

Each volume sets out the key elements of the particular method and features examples of its application, drawing on a consistent structure across the whole series. Written in an accessible style by leading experts in the field, this series is an innovative pedagogical and research resource.

Also available in the series

Diary Method, Ruth Bartlett and Christine Milligan
GIS, Nick Bearman
Inclusive Research, Melanie Nind
Qualitative Longitudinal Research, Bren Neale
Quantitative Longitudinal Data Analysis, Vernon Gayle and Paul Lambert
Rhythmanalysis, Dawn Lyon

Forthcoming in the series

Embodied Inquiry, Jennifer Leigh and Nicole Brown
Statistical Modelling in R, Kevin Ralston, Vernon Gayle, Roxanne Connelly and Chris Playford

Community

Studies

Research Methods

Graham Crow

BLOOMSBURY ACADEMIC
LONDON · NEW YORK · OXFORD · NEW DELHI · SYDNEY

BLOOMSBURY ACADEMIC
Bloomsbury Publishing Plc
50 Bedford Square, London, WC1B 3DP, UK
1385 Broadway, New York, NY 10018, USA

First published Open Access under a Creative Commons license in 2018
as *What are Community Studies?*, this title is now also available as part
of the Bloomsbury Research Methods series.
This edition published 2021

Series design by Charlotte James
Cover image © shuoshu / iStock

A catalogue record for this book is available from the British Library.

A catalog record for this book is available from the Library of Congress.

ISBN: HB: 978-1-3501-8860-0
PB: 978-1-3501-8859-4
ePDF: 978-1-3501-8862-4
eBook: 978-1-3501-8861-7

Series: Bloomsbury Research Methods

Typeset by Deanta Global Publishing Services, Chennai, India

To find out more about our authors and books visit www.bloomsbury.com
and sign up for our newsletters.

Contents

Acknowledgements

This book has benefitted greatly from collaborative writing on community over the years with Graham Allan, Nickie Charles, Jaimie Ellis, Dawn Lyon, Catherine Maclean, Alice Mah, Bethany Morgan and Marcia Summers. Thanks are also due to the publisher's anonymous referees for their helpful comments on an earlier draft. The team at Bloomsbury Academic have also provided invaluable support through keeping faith with the project and providing the advice needed to bring it to completion.

Series foreword

The idea behind this book series is a simple one: to provide concise and accessible introductions to frequently used research methods and of current issues in research methodology. Books in the series have been written by experts in their fields with a brief to write about their subject for a broad audience.

The series has been developed through a partnership between Bloomsbury and the UK's National Centre for Research Methods (NCRM). The original 'What is?' Research Methods Series sprang from the eponymous strand at NCRM's Research Methods Festivals.

This relaunched series reflects changes in the research landscape, embracing research methods innovation and interdisciplinarity. Methodological innovation is the order of the day, while still maintaining an emphasis on accessibility to a wide audience. The format allows researchers who are new to a field to gain an insight into its key features, while also providing a useful update on recent developments for people who have had some prior acquaintance with it. All readers should find it helpful to be taken through the discussion of key terms, the history of how the method or methodological issue has developed, and the assessment of the strengths and possible weaknesses of the approach through analysis of illustrative examples.

This book is devoted to community studies. In it, Graham Crow takes readers through a field of social science research which has a history going back almost one hundred years. In that time it has witnessed a number of developments and reorientations, but has always kept the core idea that the different elements of people's everyday lives are connected. The details of how these connections operate often turn out to be surprising, whether it is how information about job opportunities is shared via unexpected channels or the ways in which apparently welcoming communities can be inclusive for some people but exclusive for others. Researchers going into communities are therefore advised to proceed with an open agenda.

The serendipity that is frequently reported to have played a crucial part in arriving at the most interesting findings cannot be pre-planned – it is something that happens unexpectedly, for example through chance encounters. As a result, community studies typically employ a range of research methods as a way of investigating the subject being studied from a variety of angles. As the exemplars that are discussed in the book demonstrate, there is a place in community studies for surveys, ethnographic observation, documentary research, photography and numerous other methods to be used in creative combinations. The enduring popularity of community studies can be attributed to the richness and diversity of the findings that they present as windows onto the key part that community relationships play in shaping people's lives.

The books in this series cannot provide information about their subject matter down to a fine level of detail, but they will equip readers with a powerful sense of reasons why it deserves to be taken seriously and, it is hoped, with the enthusiasm to put that knowledge into practice.

Patrick Sturgis
London School of Economics, UK

1 Defining key terms

Defining 'community' has been a long-standing challenge. It can be readily agreed that a community involves a group of people with something in common, but it is less easy to find agreement about what that thing is. This book does not set out to solve the problem of defining 'community' to everyone's satisfaction; rather it aims to explore the many different ways in which people understand 'community', and the related variety of methodological approaches that are available to be used in studying community phenomena. Many of the most famous community studies have been undertaken using ethnographic methods that involve the researcher spending time among the people of the community under investigation, observing their behaviour and interacting with them in the conduct of their everyday lives. These studies are celebrated for their ability to capture the texture of everyday interactions, exchanges and routines. The idea of a community study as a contextualized account of ordinary people's everyday lives and of how the various elements of those lives are interconnected as parts of a larger whole provides us with a working definition. It should be emphasized, however, that ethnographic observation is by no means the only research method available to capture the stuff of community relationships, and the exemplars of community studies that will be discussed in this book have been selected with this diversity of research methods in mind. There are multiple ways of doing a community study.

This diversity of approach is a strength, not a weakness. The availability of a wide range of methods, from ethnographic observation to interviews and surveys, from photography and other visual methods to policy evaluation, from social network analysis to experiments, and from documentary analysis to online methods, means that researchers investigate community relationships from numerous angles. In terms of disciplines, community studies provide an interdisciplinary meeting place for anthropologists, educationalists, geographers, historians, psychologists, social workers, sociologists and others interested in how and why community contexts matter. This is desirable because 'community' is an elusive quarry and debates about it involve different theoretical perspectives. Communities may be associated with particular places, but they do not have to be, as reference to the geographically dispersed deaf community readily demonstrates (Gregory and Hartley 1991). Similarly, communities may comprise people with some shared identity, but pinning down what constitutes the basis of that shared identity often proves frustratingly difficult, especially at the margins of the group where it is unclear precisely who should count as an 'insider' and who an 'outsider'. Next, communities may be constellations of people with shared interests, such as the members of an occupational community (coal miners, fishermen, railway workers and architects are some of the occupational groups that have been studied in this way), but it is evident here as well that such communities built around a common interest can still be quite heterogeneous and have some members who are more active and influential than others. Communities do not come in uniform packages ready for one standardized mode of analysis.

Not all studies of communities are community studies in the sense of attempting an extensive analysis of how the various parts of community life connect. The tradition of community studies research is frequently traced back to a pioneering piece of research conducted in the 1920s by the husband and wife team of Robert and Helen Lynd in the city of Muncie, Indiana, in the United States. In this study the Lynds went beyond their original brief to investigate religion in the life of small-town middle America, and identified five other aspects of everyday life besides religion on which they also focused attention. The book quickly if surprisingly became a classic piece of popular social science. Its core sections were headed 'getting a living', 'making a home', 'training the young', 'using leisure', 'engaging in religious practices' and 'engaging in community activities'. This list of topics, which we can condense into work, home, education, leisure, religion and community action, has become familiar in community studies. Many researchers have sought to follow the Lynds in tracing the interconnectedness of the various elements of community life. *Middletown* (the pseudonym that they gave to Muncie) is a key point of reference for community studies scholars, and the town and its people continue to attract academic interest, as we shall see in one of the exemplars of community research considered in Chapter 3. Beyond 'Muncieology', as this body of research is known, many ethnographers continue to use variations on the format of the six broad topics on which the Lynds focused nearly a century ago. Community studies do not have to be this ambitious, however; researchers are tending to concentrate on a narrower brief.

The connectedness of community life is often understood as underpinning the social solidarity of community members. The Lynds (1929: ch.XXVIII) used this concept, as did Alwyn Rees (1951) analysing kinship ties, Gerald Suttles (1972) studying neighbourhoods, Arlie Hochschild (1973) observing residential settings, Philip Abrams and Andrew McCulloch (1976) investigating communes, Graeme Salaman (1986) looking at occupational communities, David Rayside (1991) examining small-town change and many others (Crow 2002a). Social solidarity expresses a shared sense of belonging and commitment among community members; it is what differentiates community from an agglomeration of people who lack a firm basis for existing as an entity in which co-operation, mutual aid and reciprocity are practised. The abstract concept of social solidarity is not easy to operationalize in empirical research, however (Bulmer 1986: 34). In part as a response to this problem, alternative concepts have been developed to capture the idea of communities as groups of people bound together in some way (despite their myriad differences of social class, age, gender, disability and other lines of social cleavage). These include social capital, community cohesion, communities of practice and social networks. A common thread running through these ideas is the notion that being among 'people like us' (or 'people like ourselves') matters and is worth seeking out for the benefits it brings.

The connectedness of people's lives as workmates, family members, neighbours, schoolmates, friends, members of leisure groups, members of religious organizations and community activists is at the heart of conventional communities of place, in which roles and networks inevitably tend to overlap. Any individual relationship between two community members is unlikely to exist in isolation, but rather will be linked into wider webs of sociability that reinforce each other as common bonds and provide a basis for shared identity and action. It has been argued that such solidarities are the strongest where people are brought together by shared poverty and need for assistance – what Raymond Williams called 'the mutuality of the oppressed' (1975: 131) – but as Williams himself notes, there are many examples of active community solidarities outside of those conditions. Nor should it be concluded that poverty always stimulates social solidarity among members of groups faced with limited material resources; the dynamics of such situations are more complex than that. Social solidarity is one possible outcome, but domination and control of poor populations is another (Brent 2009: 18).

Ethnography has provided a particularly fruitful methodological approach in community studies. Only through participant observation will some aspects of the incredible complexity of ordinary people's everyday lives become apparent. Elements of community life may be hidden from researchers as they would be from any outsiders, due to mistrust; suspicion of being a spy or informant has been reported numerous times (Crow and Pope 2008). It takes time for the presence of researchers to be accepted. Periods of fieldwork may last for years or even decades (Crow 2000: 181), for reasons of trust-building and also because the meaning of mundane everyday activities may not be immediately apparent to either researchers or community members (Goffman 2002). Everyday practices are an important part of how communities function, but they may be too familiar to community members and too apparently insignificant to observers for their significance to be appreciated. It takes time to see things in proper perspective, and to know what to look out for. Participation in community life adds to researchers' observations by giving them more of a 'feel' of what being part of a community is like. Recent reflections by researchers about the practice of research have led to growing interest in sensory ethnography and the breadth of ways in which the phenomena under investigation may be captured by researchers (Pink 2009). This development also reveals the more general point that ethnographic methods do not stand still, but evolve as new ways of thinking emerge about how best to undertake research.

Two further points stand out in respect of recent developments in the methods used in community research. One is that the merits of adopting a mixed-methods approach to the study of community relationships are becoming more widely appreciated. Communities are multifaceted phenomena; it follows that it is unlikely that one research tool will capture this multifacetedness as effectively as an approach in which a combination of methods is employed. The exemplars of community studies that will be examined in Chapter 3 are all pieces of mixed-methods research whose authors recognize that different methods are necessary in order to get at formal and informal relationships, open and hidden, episodic and enduring, consensual and conflictual, sacred and profane, or mythical and real. A photograph may capture some aspect of community life that a person being interviewed could find it difficult to put into words.

A social network analysis may highlight connections and cleavages that conventional mapping of where different social groups reside might miss. And documentary analysis of archived material may cast a quite different light on matters than oral history testimony does. When used together, these methods can provide a much more rounded account of community life than any on its own would be able to, and although different methods always have the potential to generate apparently contradictory results, further analysis has the potential to resolve such issues.

This ties in with the second point about recent developments, the growing tendency for community research to be undertaken collaboratively, with researchers and community members working together in a shared enterprise (Campbell and Lassiter 2014). Collaborative ethnography provides one of the exemplars considered in Chapter 3. The rationale for doing ethnography in this way is instructive: it is framed in terms of granting respect to members of communities that are being researched, recognizing that research has the potential to be intrusive, and to involve costs to participants in terms of time and other things. With these considerations in mind, it is only fair that community members should have a say in what is to be researched, and how it is to be researched, as well as being able at least to ask, 'What are the potential benefits to arise through the publication of research findings?' Put simply, people being researched deserve a voice in the research process. Alongside this set of ethical arguments there is another set of considerations which points in the same direction but on more pragmatic grounds. Without access to consenting community members there can be little if any research, so working with them to secure their agreement to be studied has always been a point to bear in mind. Similarly, willing participants in research are more likely than reluctant ones to provide better quality data, and to be more effective partners in the dissemination of research findings. Researchers thus have a degree of self-interest in working collaboratively, and also in managing expectations about what research achieves; experience teaches us that over-promising about the benefits of research is something that it is important to avoid (Crow 2013).

Community studies is thus a field of research in which there is a recognizable tradition that at the same time has not stood still. Community studies are studies of communities that may be geographically based but do not have to be, because communities are constructed around a number of characteristics that people share, of which place is only one.

Community studies have the potential to focus on a range of aspects of everyday life, from youth to religion, work to home and politics to leisure, but always with an emphasis on the importance of the wider context in which the chosen subjects are to be understood. Ethnographic methods of participant observation are particularly widely used as a route into exploring the interconnectedness of the different aspects of community life, but they can be supplemented by many other methods such as surveys, elite interviews, life histories, visual methods and documentary analysis that also have the potential to capture the realities of ordinary people's everyday lives (Davies 1999; Payne and Payne 2004: 46–50). The Marienthal study in 1930s Austria famously used diary methods and essays imagining the future (Jahoda, Lazarsfeld and Zeisel 1972). Tony Blackshaw (2010) has added action research, community profiling and social network analysis to the list. Jeremy Brent's (2009) inclusion of autobiographical material brings another dimension, as does Daniel Nettle's (2015) use of experiments. It should be noted that whichever of these methods are used, the ideal of researching ethically always requires attention. The history of community studies includes salutary stories where standards of behaviour have fallen short of what is desirable as well as cases of exemplary achievements that have become the landmarks of research in the community studies tradition. This history is the subject of the next chapter.

2 A history

2.1 Starting points and forerunners

The Lynds in 1920s America were the first researchers to produce a recognizable community study in the modern format, but *Middletown* was far from being the first piece of social scientific research into community matters. Close by (both geographically and in time) a distinct body of work that would later become known as the Chicago School was already taking form as the sociologists in that city followed the exhortation of Robert Park, a journalist turned sociologist, to learn about the various phenomena of urban life through street-level observation and spending time close to the people being researched. It was the antithesis of so-called 'armchair sociology' (Smith 1988: 102). By the end of the 1920s, a wealth of studies had already been published on gangs, tramps, migration, ethnic segregation, delinquency and the contrasting lifestyles of the inhabitants of rich and poor areas of the city. As a result, more was known about Chicago than anywhere else (Stein 1964: 13). Taken together, these reports revealed the city to be like an organism with its spatially discrete but nevertheless interconnected parts. Park and his collaborator Roderick McKenzie coined the term 'human ecology' to highlight the relationship of communities to their environment (Park 1952), expressing the enduring if contested idea that there is something natural about communities (Suttles 1972: ch.1). This did not mean that communities had to be accepted as they were. Dennis Smith (1988) rightly assessed the Chicago School to have advanced 'a liberal critique of capitalism'. This is quite consistent with Park's view of the city as a social laboratory where experiments in ways of living were taking place, out of which new forms of community could emerge.

Various research-based social interventions intended to bring about improvements in people's welfare had prominence in Chicago from the late nineteenth century. These projects have had a lasting impact on the field of social work studies in the same way that the Chicago School has provided a defining point of reference for sociology. That disciplinary distinction was not as evident at the time as it has later become, and the association of women with welfare projects was only part of the story; the focus on this aspect has diverted attention from the achievements of Jane Addams and other women as social theorists and methodologists as well as practical reformers (McDonald 1994: 228–33; Platt 1996: 262). This outpouring of research activity in Chicago deserves explanation. There was something about the speed with which the city had developed that facilitated scrutiny of its operation – Max Weber on a visit there in 1904 commented that it was a city whose inner workings could be observed 'like a man whose skin has been peeled off and whose intestines are seen at work' (Weber 1988: 286–7) – and there was a corresponding urgency about finding solutions to its many evident social problems. The rawness of these problems sat uneasily alongside the city's growing 'cultural confidence' (Bulmer 1984: 14), making for a heady mix.

Chicago was also a city whose profile corresponded to the issues of theoretical debate that were being identified by early social scientists in the United States and elsewhere, particularly Germany, among whose authors Georg Simmel and his ideas on adjustment to city life had especial resonance. The development of industrial cities prompted the idea that contemporary urban life was of a different form to life in rural locations, and the recruitment to the cities of people from the countryside meant that this contrast was very real for migrants. This was famously true for the people studied in *The Polish Peasant in Europe and America*, whose migration had an additional cross-cultural dimension to it. The authors of this work, William Thomas and Florian Znaniecki, claimed that personal documents such as letters constituted 'perfect' sociological material, although the life histories that these documents made it possible to construct were not necessarily representative of wider populations (Madge 1970: 61). This issue of the typicality or atypicality of cases is one that continually resurfaces in the history of community research, not least because the vividness of material relating to individual cases makes it attractive to use precisely because its unusualness brings with it an element of surprise.

The conclusion towards which the Chicago researchers from the late nineteenth century onwards pointed was that modern cities needed to be studied because they were not only new in the form that they took, but also potentially unstable. This instability made them dangerous, both to their inhabitants through their poor living conditions and to the social order through the more limited social support and looser social control that was thought to exist there. In this context it was understandable that urban life with its mobility and fluidity would come to be associated with an absence of community compared to the fixity and familiarity of rural communities, although in time the loss of community theme would also come to be associated with the countryside as well, as communities there saw population decline and growing urban cultural influences. Louis Wirth provided a key expression of these ideas of community taking different forms in cities and the countryside in his classic paper 'urbanism as a way of life'. In his view, cities took people away from 'natural' situations: 'Nowhere has mankind been further removed from organic nature than under the conditions of life characteristic of great cities' (1938: 1–2). This perspective paved the way for rural–urban and urban–suburban contrasts that have been significant in the history of community studies (as have later reactions to them, to be discussed below).

In Britain where the first industrial nation was forged, the urban transformation took place sooner than in the United States and continental Europe; so did pioneering social research into life in urban communities. Among these pioneers Friedrich Engels stands out as an early illustration of the power of reporting on life as it takes place all around the attentive researcher who is minded to look behind facades. His account in *The Condition of the Working Class in England* revealed 1840s Manchester where he lived and worked to be a world of both prosperity and squalor, inextricably linked. London attracted more extensive investigation from researchers located in contrasting philosophical and political traditions who employed a variety of methods, including large-scale quantitative studies of poverty conducted over many years as well as more literary evocations (Crow 2014). At times the political purpose underlying studies of Victorian London and other cities found expression in judgemental narratives that arose from the tensions between what was discovered and what the researcher felt to be desirable. But whatever personal motivations the researchers had, they were united in believing in the value of research to reveal uncomfortable hidden realities to which complacent inactivity was not an acceptable response.

Social researchers who were also social reformers saw research as a vehicle for promoting social improvement through community development, but their choice of methods and theories used to study communities could be idiosyncratic. This criticism has been made of the extensive body of research projects associated with Patrick Geddes and his early-twentieth-century followers, whose openness to diverse and sometimes contradictory influences led to accounts of community that were at once social, economic, geographical, biological and architectural, and also empirical and utopian, combined in something of a melange. This was compounded by the reliance on local volunteers rather than trained social scientists to undertake the surveys, with predictably uneven outcomes (Kent 1981). However well-intentioned, such research was open to criticism for its amateurism. In the disillusionment that followed the failure of such research to deliver sustained social improvement, community research took a different direction, although some elements of Geddes and his colleagues' approach survived. These include the key tenet that place, work, family and community life are all combined in reciprocal relationships (Savage and Warde 1993: 20), and the practice of seeking an overview of a district from a high vantage point, inspired by the panorama of Edinburgh gained from the Outlook Tower (Scott and Bromley 2013: 96; Crow 2000). These elements were compatible with more inductive approaches that came to the fore around the middle of the twentieth century in what may be considered a golden age for community studies, or at least community studies of a particular type.

2.2 The rise and fall of classic community studies

The third quarter of the twentieth century witnessed a remarkable profusion of detailed ethnographic studies of diverse places and the people who lived there. The way for this development had been paved by various landmark projects, including three pioneering studies conducted in rural communities in different national contexts outside of the United States and the United Kingdom: Robert Redfield's *Tepoztlán – A Mexican Village*, Conrad Arensberg and Solon Kimball's *Family and Community in Ireland* and Everett Hughes's *French Canada in Transition* (published in 1930, 1940 and 1943, respectively). The authors of the first and third of these came out of the Chicago School and their contrasting styles illustrate the breadth of that inheritance, while the second was different again, drawing inspiration from Lloyd Warner's *Yankee City* research on Newburyport in New England (Bell and Newby 1974: 42), which was more reliant on the use of quantitative methods as part of a mixed-methods approach (Warner and Lunt 1941: ch. III). Despite their differences, all of them sought to record

in detail the way of life of people in rural communities, with the anthro-
pologist's concern to capture how core social institutions worked from the
point of view of participants in those institutions. The elaboration of such
internal points of view had the potential to surprise those outsiders who
lazily assumed the universality of their familiar, fixed way of understanding
the world.

The rural community studies of the mid-twentieth-century generation pursued a variety of themes, including the contentious one of social
divisions in ostensibly contented communities. The title of E. W. Martin's
(1965) study *The Shearers and the Shorn* echoes Talleyrand to make this
point. Such studies served to highlight how community members are
divided (often materially) despite their commonalities, and united (often
symbolically) despite their inequalities (Crow and Maclean 2013). Set in
Wales, Ronald Frankenberg's *Village on the Border* (published in 1957)
recorded how social divisions were not only a feature of collective life,
but also integral to it. In this early example of 'anthropology at home'
(Jackson 1987), Frankenberg explored the position of 'strangers' through
his own involvement in community life as a non-Welsh outsider. He later
recounted: 'In my early days in the village I would often climb a hill and
look sadly down upon the rows of houses of the housing estate and
wonder what went on inside them' (1969: 16). The research progressed
once Frankenberg became involved in village activities, which in turn shed
light on what he called (in a phrase borrowing from Bronislaw Malinowski
designed to convey the inherent strangeness of other people's cultures)
'the imponderabilia of everyday life' (1990: 177). Not least among these
issues was the role that outsiders may be called upon to play in the resolu-
tion of disputes between community insiders.

Another rural study to break new ground was Alwyn Rees's *Life in a
Welsh Countryside*, a book that gives a strong sense of place and people
through its inclusion of photographs, maps, figures and diagrams. These
include a representation of the network of kinship ties between households in which the connecting lines are so dense that the local expression
of these resembling 'a pig's entrails' (1951: 75–6) makes immediate sense.
Nigel Rapport later found this idea echoed in his own fieldwork in Cumbria,
where the local expression had it that 'Kick one person from Wanet and
next day seven people will be limping' (1993: 43), and a similar expression
is reported for Swansea (Rosser and Harris 1965: 5). The use of visual methods and social network analysis in Rees's study may be rudimentary by

today's standards, but the important thing to note is the fact that they are there at all; they serve as a corrective against those myopic narratives of methodological innovation that neglect this history. It is telling, however, that the network map of kinship ties stops at the parish boundaries and gives an impression of the community as a self-contained unit. In practice, local autonomy was fast being eroded, as Rees's reference to 'the impact of modern industrial and urban civilisation' (1951: 164) conceded.

This theme of the encroachment of the wider society into rural community life was central to Arthur Vidich and Joseph Bensman's *Small Town in Mass Society*, a study of a rural community in upstate New York. One of the purposes of community studies is to act as 'gauges of change' (Hughes 1971: 76), and the study of 'Springdale' (Vidich and Bensman's pseudonym for the community they were studying) was undertaken mindful of agriculture's declining proportion of the workforce and the rise of urban influences on rural communities. The resultant book, first published in 1958, has been much-discussed because of the hostile reception it received, including the townspeople hanging effigies of the researchers. The project's impact has been enduring because the ethics of gaining access to a community by promising something more positive than it is actually possible to deliver has ongoing relevance (Crow 2013). Also of enduring significance for the practice of community studies is the way in which Vidich and Bensman sought out as key respondents 'individuals who are socially marginal in the society being studied' (2000: 354). People working in professions such as journalism and teaching will typically be less-firmly incorporated into mainstream local culture and less persuaded by widely held beliefs about its superiority over other ways of life. By adopting their more critical stance on Springdale's view of itself, and treating local beliefs as 'myths', the book's authors were set on a collision course with their hosts, a problem compounded by Vidich and Bensman's (1971) subsequent characterization of the townspeople as 'sensitive'. Any future research in the town was rendered impossible.

The same theme of the incorporation of people and places into the wider society was pursued as well in research into suburbia. J. R. Seeley and his colleagues' *Crestwood Heights* presents it as a depiction of community life, but it is a community that exists only because of its relationship to 'Big City' (in fact Toronto, Canada). The relationship was treated as psychologically important, with the city providing a point of comparison that allowed the residents of Crestwood Heights to feel superior. In this respect there was a parallel with the prevailing belief in Springdale of the town being a desirable place to live, but the grounding of such beliefs could not be the same since Crestwood Heights as a new community lacked history. Its functioning as a community had instead to be attributed to 'the relationships that exist between people – relationships revealed in the functioning of the institutions which they have created: family, school, church, community center, club, association, summer camp'. Suburban developments brought together populations of strangers, and constituted something of an 'experiment' (1963: 4, 431). In the case of Crestwood Heights, not only did residents arrive not knowing their new neighbours, they also were aware that their new location was impermanent because of the periodic geographical mobility that accompanied their middle-class lifestyles. Suburbanization might be expected to bring with it anonymization and fragmentation rather than the successful creation of communities, and the discovery to the contrary in this and other studies of suburbia (such as Herbert Gans's (1967) *The Levittowners* and Suzanne Keller's (2003) report on Twin Rivers, New Jersey) posed a fundamental challenge to theories of community reliant on the idea that geographical location has a determining influence on social life.

Gans had already grappled with the issue of the relationship of community to place, both theoretically (1962a) and in his account of the dense patterns of social relationships found among Italian Americans in a slum area of Boston, Massachusetts, prior to its demolition. His book's title, *The Urban Villagers* (Gans 1962b), conveyed the paradoxical nature of the phenomenon, at least from the point of view that associated urban life with atrophied forms of community. In the UK various studies were arriving at similar conclusions, the most widely read of these being Michael Young and Peter Willmott's (1957) *Family and Kinship in East London*, which discovered the very opposite of urban anonymity and social fracture at the heart of this global city. Colin Rosser and Christopher Harris (1965) painted a similar picture for urban life in Swansea in *The Family and Social Change*, even as its population became more mobile, both socially and geographically. It fell to Ray Pahl to pull all of these strands together and draw the inevitable conclusion to which they and his own research on commuters who lived in rural settings north of London (Pahl 1965) pointed that 'any attempt to tie particular patterns of social relationships to specific geographical milieux is a singularly fruitless exercise' (1968: 293). If the classic occupational community, that of Yorkshire coalminers as studied by Norman Dennis and his colleagues (1969) in *Coal Is Our Life*, had to be interpreted as 'the town that is a village' (Frankenberg 1969: ch.5), then it was clear that the time had come to abandon the idea, embodied in a 'rural-urban continuum', of there being a deterministic relationship between the size and density of settlement patterns and distinct types of urban and rural community relationships.

Some researchers in the field of community drew even more radical conclusions than Pahl. Margaret Stacey's first study of Banbury, a market town in the English midlands, had taken the Lynds' *Middletown* as a point of reference (Stacey 1960: v) and she was engaged in working on a restudy when she concluded that 'it is doubtful that the concept "community" refers to a useful abstraction' (1969: 134). Coming at the end of a decade which had seen the publication of numerous influential community studies, including her own, this statement represented a serious loss of faith in the wider project of capturing the social world through this genre of research. Her concerns were both theoretical and methodological. She argued that 'community' was difficult if not impossible to isolate in research into how societies work, and proposed instead using the concept of 'local social system' as the basis for developing testable hypotheses. This strategy offered a way out of the problem of community studies being unable to progress beyond individual insights into a coherent incremental body of knowledge. For the field to develop through accumulating knowledge, some way of comparing studies would be required; as she expressed it, 'A highly idiosyncratic non-replicable study may be seminal, but cannot be used comparatively' (1969: 138). The Banbury restudy was eventually published (Stacey et al. 1975), but it was one of the last community studies conceived in what can be called, following Jennifer Platt (1971: ch.3), the 'old tradition'. It would be superseded after a hiatus by a rejuvenated form in which confidence about the value of 'community' as a focus of inquiry had returned, along with revised methodological practices that could meet the criticisms of community studies as insufficiently theoretically informed and overly concerned with small-scale, local issues in a way that left the impact of larger social and economic forces unaddressed.

The work of the Institute of Community Studies ICS embodies in miniature this phase of the genre's evolution, in which remarkable success was followed by doubt and reassessment. Founded in 1953 by the social entrepreneur Michael Young (Briggs 2001: 6), the ICS is most famous for his and his colleague Peter Willmott's best-selling *Family and Kinship in*

East London (Young and Willmott 1957), which reported on the continuing importance of community ties in the age of the welfare state. Further
studies by numerous ICS authors followed, covering a range of topics
(including widowhood, mental illness, medical services, education and
social mobility, youth and urban planning) that arguably matched the
breadth of scope of the early Chicago School, all emphasizing the importance of community context, although not all of them involved fieldwork
in East London. These projects were deliberately framed as social research
with a purpose, to promote social awareness and social change; that is,
they embodied an ethos of engagement with the wider public as well
as policy makers. Platt's (1971) evaluation of this body of work was that
engagement with diverse audiences came at a cost: opportunities for
methodological innovation were not always taken up, and in presentation
there was a tendency towards an 'impressionistic' style, a word also used
in Richard Titmuss's foreword to the first edition of *Family and Kinship*
(perhaps explaining why the foreword did not appear in subsequent edi-
tions). Put another way, questions were being raised about the rigour of
the ICS's way of working.

Jocelyn Cornwell's (1984) return to Bethnal Green highlighted the way in
which the public celebration of 'community' was one side of a coin which
could lead to the less attractive reverse side of private narratives (in which
violence and snobbery also figured) being overlooked. Only by penetrat-
ing behind the public face of community myths of positive togetherness
could a more balanced assessment of the traditional working-class community be gained. Geoff Payne's question about community studies which
Family and Kinship epitomized, why do they 'seem so full of such *nice*
people?' (1996: 18, emphasis in original), is answered partly by the failure to
penetrate behind myths, and partly by selectivity (conscious or otherwise)
in decisions about which members of communities to consult. When
researchers at the Young Foundation (which the ICS became) undertook
a restudy of *Family and Kinship*, other charges would be levelled at their
book (Dench, Gavron and Young 2006), but not ones of looking at things
through rose-tinted spectacles or of failure to speak to 'missing' sections
of the study population. This was a key point of criticism of mid-century
community studies: that they were vulnerable to being partial in their
coverage. In some, women's voices went unheard, or were misheard, and
misrepresented, by male researchers; the best-known community studies
were among these (Frankenberg 1976). Similar points were made about

how in other studies different groups' voices came to be marginalized. These criticisms required researchers to pay attention to the lessons this entailed for the research methods employed and to the operationalization of the term 'community' using researchers' chosen tools.

2.3 Reconsideration and renewal

Rethinking the way in which community was researched necessarily entailed theoretical debate about the concept of community. A key reference point that had been published in German in 1887 but was not available in an English translation until 1955 was *Community and Association* by Ferdinand Tönnies. The reduction of the distinction between two antipathetic types of social arrangements, *gemeinschaft* and *gesellschaft*, to a contrast between small rural and large urban settlements lost much of the subtlety of what Tönnies had to say about the erosion by social and economic forces of the enduring connections to and consequent intimate knowledge of others that came from living in close-knit social worlds (Lee and Newby 1983: Part 2). Industrializing and urbanizing societies were becoming less 'organic' and more 'mechanical' (Tönnies 1955: 39), and as a result communities' religious, work, family and cultural traditions were transformed. Interestingly, Tönnies' contemporary Emile Durkheim borrowed and reworked the concepts of mechanical and organic solidarity, and through his account of social change challenged the notion that the conditions of modern social life ruled out the intense social bonds that Tönnies treated as beleaguered (Crow 2005). By the early 1970s the ensuing debate was focussing on whether using the concept of community implied acceptance of Tönnies's nostalgia that appealed to readers who longed to see 'a return to an earlier stage in the development of societies where life was simpler' (Elias 1974: xi). This debate has continued down to the present, for example in the work of Zygmunt Bauman (2001).

The renewed attention being paid to the theory of community had powerful consequences. Engagement with theoretical ideas was necessary because community studies were being characterized by critics as descriptive, capable of portraying communities but not explaining them. It was partly as a response to this criticism that Stacey looked to theory to help frame an approach that would get beyond fact-finding about social problems and capture a fuller understanding of the dynamics of ordinary life including everyday routines as well as the pursuit of power and status (Savage 2010: 151). Meanwhile, critics of the tendency to romanticize community relationships that characterized the work of the ICS arrived by a different route at the same conclusion, that communities were about competition and conflict as well as co-operation, and these phenomena needed in particular to be explained as something other than expressions of exceptional, aberrant social forces. Supporters of this line of reasoning could refer to John Rex and Robert Moore's path-breaking *Race, Community and Conflict* as an example of the sort of research results that could be achieved by dropping the assumption that communities were consensual and adopting instead a conflict perspective. By the 1960s immigration from overseas into cities like Birmingham was resulting in intense competition over resources such as housing, and the Sparkbrook study drew successfully on the Chicago School's model of differentiated urban zones, occupied by subcommunities brought together around ethnic and racial identities. Spatial segregation along ethnic lines meant that there were 'three Sparkbrooks' (1967: ch.II), not one. Here, and elsewhere, research was highlighting that an administrative boundary could contain more than one community.

First published in 1965, Norbert Elias and John Scotson's (1994) study of the 'Winston Parva' neighbourhood of Leicester offered a different explanation of the same scenario, a bounded geographical area split into a hierarchy of residential groups whose members related to others with a combination of stereotype-based discrimination and fear. A shared identity was strikingly absent in both Sparkbrook and Winston Parva. Across the Atlantic, Gerald Suttles (1968) was retracing themes of the Chicago School in the area of that city where Addams had been active in seeking to combat social problems three quarters of a century earlier. This slum neighbourhood was characterized by a pattern of separation between different racial and ethnic groups, which, despite being marked by conflict, was orderly. Suttles found solidarity between ethnic group members, and separate, 'provincial' cultures which were reproduced through social processes such as gossip (which Elias and Scotson had also highlighted in their study) to sustain a 'moral order'. Despite expectations to the contrary held by outsider observers, slum areas were characterized by social order, just not the type that was usually associated with that term. Alice Goffman's study of Philadelphia as home to 'a community on the run' (2014: xii) is a recent expression of this tradition of research finding shared identity and norms of behaviour and even solidarity among a disadvantaged group frequently subject to misunderstanding by outsiders.

As previous thinking about the relationship of community to space was criticized and the association of community with consensus was challenged by researchers whose work highlighted conflict, community studies went out of fashion for a time. Awareness that local distinctiveness was being eroded by large-scale secular forces such as bureaucratization led some commentators to suggest that the phenomenon of community was in the process of being eclipsed (Stein 1964). For others the very concept of 'community' was an object of attack for glossing over and thereby concealing the presence of inequalities of social class, gender, and race and ethnicity. Graham Day's useful account of community studies up to this point treats the 1960s as a decade in which a crisis point was reached from which it was difficult for the genre to recover (2006: ch.2). It is certainly true that few community studies were published in the 1970s, although pointers to themes that would figure prominently in the rejuvenation of the field that was to come can be detected among those few that were (Bulmer 1985: 431). There is a political edge to Ken Coates and Richard Silburn's (1973) study of poverty and housing decay set in the context of inner-city Nottingham, while Ken Pryce's (1979) *Endless Pressure* explored ethnic minority alienation in another British inner-city context, Bristol. In Australia, the gap between suburban promise and reality was the setting for Lois Bryson and Faith Thompson's (1972) analysis of the reproduction of class inequalities, while in the United States Albert Hunter's (1974) work in Chicago emphasized the importance of community symbols. All of these studies in their different ways made the case for holding on to a focus on community phenomena which continued to have real significance in ordinary people's everyday lives. Arguably this was not despite the growing significance of wider influences on communities, but because of them. People looked to 'community' as a source of support and of meaning precisely as community boundaries were being traversed as never before.

Since 1980, criticisms of community studies as backward-looking nostalgic celebrations of disappearing ways of life have been met by numerous studies of contemporary community which are anything but nostalgic. As Robert Burgess has noted, 'The ethnographer no longer focuses merely on the exotic and the obscure in societies other than our own' (2001: 38), but is increasingly found investigating familiar phenomena closer to home. In anthropology, Anthony Cohen has highlighted the importance of communities' symbolic boundaries in the context of it becoming ever more apparent that complete self-containment for communities is impossible in the modern world. Cohen's (1987) own work on *Whalsay* in Shetland is part of a much broader body of research in relatively remote locations (Cohen 1982, 1986), but similar themes about the constructed and negotiated character of boundaries also emerge from research conducted in the heart of great cities. Here long-established themes of spatial boundaries of inclusion and exclusion that can be traced back to the Chicago School continue to generate 'turf wars' (Modan 2007). In some exclusive contexts boundaries are managed through the device of 'gated communities' (Low 2003), in others there are more subtle mechanisms by which the desire to live among 'people like us' is pursued (Butler with Robson 2003; Savage, Bagnall and Longhurst 2005). These and other studies such as Keller's (2003) research into a suburban development reveal that the pursuit of the dream of community often involves geographical mobility.

The growth of people's spatial movement anticipated in Colin Rosser and Christopher Harris's (1965: ch.1) notion of 'the mobile society' is a prominent theme of recent restudies. Janet Foster's (1999) *Docklands* involves a return to the east end of London, and stands out as a study of 'worlds in collision' as people, ideas and practices from around the globe are brought together in new configurations. Other studies of this area also highlight the movement of people and its effect of 'changing places' (Mumford and Power 2003: ch.10), including what some see as the loss of the 'brief golden age' (Dench, Gavron and Young 2006: 20) that had been celebrated in Young and Willmott's original research. Restudies of classic community studies do not have to be conducted in exactly the same way and with precisely the same conceptual frameworks as the originals in order to illuminate the process of social change; rather, they are stronger for looking at old themes afresh (Charles and Crow 2012; Hammersley 2016). These themes of the erosion of isolation, the significance of geographical mobility, and the lessons to be learned about communities through restudies have influenced the selection of exemplars of recent community studies, which will be focused on in the next chapter. These exemplars have been selected to convey the vitality of community research as researchers have responded imaginatively to the critique of 'the old tradition' in order to better capture how as some forms of community decline, others emerge.

3 Three exemplars

It is somewhat arbitrary to take 1980 as the start of a new period of community studies research, but not entirely. The need for a fresh beginning had been encapsulated in Philip Abrams's observation that the field was marked by the paradoxical 'coexistence of a body of theory which constantly predicts the collapse of community and a body of empirical studies which finds community alive and well' (1978: 12). Abrams himself was immersed in empirical research into community relationships involving neighbours as these words were being published (Bulmer 1986), and at the same time the fieldwork for the first exemplar to be considered in this chapter was commencing. Ray Pahl had been seeking a location to conduct his planned research into the informal economy, and in 1978 he resolved that the Isle of Sheppey in Kent met his and his funder's requirements. With that decision, a period of six years of intensive fieldwork began that resulted in *Divisions of Labour*. It has been selected partly because Pahl wanted to do something other than a traditional community study, and because in doing so he broke new ground in the combination of research methods employed by him and his team.

The chapter will then go on to consider Karen O'Reilly's *The British on the Costa del Sol*, which she undertook single-handedly as a PhD student. She later returned to the fieldwork site to conduct follow-up investigations. Her study takes further the investigation of the changing relationship between community and place in an age of unprecedented geographical mobility, and again is characterized by preparedness to innovate both conceptually and methodologically in the context of studying people's active pursuit of the dream of community. The third exemplar to be considered is Luke Eric Lassiter and his colleagues' *The Other Side of Middletown*, which is included because it facilitates a discussion of the issues raised in the conduct of a restudy – the Lynds' *Middletown* research being the original point of reference – and because it exemplifies the collaborative approach that was mentioned in Chapter 1. Together the three studies considered in this chapter are intended to give a flavour of the many ways in which community researchers have responded to the challenges laid down by the critics of the community studies tradition.

3.1 *Divisions of Labour*

The genesis of Pahl's *Divisions of Labour* is worth noting, because the project became considerably more ambitious in scope than the original research design. Starting out with only a vague notion that 'work' in its broader sense was being transformed by the growth of informality in how things get done and how people 'get by', Pahl's interest in everyday life had a special twist in the context of levels of unemployment and inflation that were taking people into unfamiliar territory. He rightly appreciated that such changes would have a marked impact on male industrial workers made redundant by the accompanying process of deindustrialization, although he was seriously wide of the mark in his initial speculation that equivalent opportunities for informal economic activity would open up for them. Even had it not been erroneous, the idea that people could respond to changed economic circumstances by engaging in practices of questionable legality (such as working informally for 'cash in hand' payment) meant that the identifiability of study participants would be an ongoing challenge. Pahl had the option of anonymizing his study area, and was still doing so as late as 1982 when he spoke of 'a local labour market on the Kent side of the Thames estuary, which has a long tradition of seasonal unemployment' (1982: 91). As time went on and the distinctiveness of the location became ever more apparent, so did the impracticality of disguising it in the book. Naming Sheppey as the fieldwork site did naturally carry some risk of some community members who had participated in the study being identifiable, at least to other community members to whom they would be instantly recognizable, but the participants were either not named or given pseudonyms, and this afforded them more protection than in some cases they wished to have.

Being an island meant that Sheppey offered an apparently self-contained community of 33,000 people whose fortunes had been tied to the occupational community associated with the Admiralty dockyard over several centuries. The closure of this dockyard in 1960 and its impact on the people of the island was still a focal point of discussions two decades later, and Pahl described conversations that he had with local residents as lay versions of the sociological perspective on social solidarity rooted in Durkheim's ideas. In these narratives the 'strong sense of social cohesion' (1984: 186) that the dockyard community had engendered became atrophied, and people's collective identity was undermined. Pahl had a long-standing interest in the way that connections to 'people like us' (1972: 83) play a pivotal role in shaping social life, as well as in community research more generally (Crow and Takeda 2011), and he was receptive to the argument that associated the weakening of collective identities with a loss of purpose and sense of direction at an individual level. As the research proceeded, he discovered unexpected things, such as that two-fifths of the island's households at the time of the study had moved there since 1960 (1984: 193), which meant that the local population was far more mobile than the imagery of 'islanders born and bred' suggested. The chapter devoted to 'myth and reality in Sheppey in the 1980s' (1984: ch.7) thus serves a useful purpose in the study, just as the myth/reality contrast has been useful in other community studies (see Berger 1968: ch.1; Keller 2003). Pahl's interest in the island was also related to the fact that it had both urban and rural characteristics, and so reinforced his scepticism (noted in Chapter 2) that places could be located on a rural–urban continuum.

An early part of Pahl's fieldwork on Sheppey involved the collection of essays written by young people in which they were invited to imagine their lives to come. Over 140 of these imagined futures essays were collected, and they sensitized Pahl to several things about the local community. These included the distinctive culture of individualism and self-reliance that instilled a degree of optimism that was arguably not warranted in the context of bleaker economic circumstances than those that had been faced by the young people's parents as they entered adulthood (Pahl 1978). Pahl certainly encountered this resilient culture among the adults with whom he spoke in his early ethnographic fieldwork, and was so struck by it that his initial speculation was that people were responding to unemployment by devising alternative ways of 'getting by'. This fitted with the broad historical sweep of his perspective which saw the reliance of households on a male breadwinner in full-time employment as a relatively recent and arguably unsustainable innovation. Informal conversations with Islanders appeared to support the argument that there were viable other ways of making a living and that the economic crisis was ushering in new patterns of working, including a revised division of labour between men and women, as part of a more general 'quiet revolution in everyday life' (1984: 200). The fact that the people of Sheppey were not typical of the wider society did not matter in this respect; indeed, the opportunity that they presented of studying the effects of deindustrialization 'in a particularly extreme form' (1984: 195) added to the location's attraction. Sheppey could be regarded as a type of laboratory, or at least 'a test case' (1984: 145), because if the much-discussed development of informal work were to be found anywhere it would be here.

The next element in Pahl's study forced a fundamental reassessment of his initial take on Sheppey life. He had been well aware of the criticism that ethnographic researchers could be vulnerable to hearing rosier views of communities than the reality justified, and the survey of one in nine of Sheppey's households confirmed a harsher message than his pilot study's thirty interviews had suggested. There are two reasons for this discrepancy between the findings generated by the two methods. One is that surveys are more trustworthy as a means of accessing a representative sample than are connections made through ethnographic fieldwork; the latter has the potential to produce findings that are skewed in various ways in terms of who participates (Payne 1996). The second reason is that surveys like the one that Pahl commissioned on Sheppey are more structured in the format of questions put to research participants than are ethnographic conversations, and this structuring of the research encounter gives survey researchers confidence that they are getting at what people do in their lives rather than what they take to be socially acceptable answers that a researcher will want to hear or be impressed by. Once the quantitative data on households' divisions of labour had been analysed, a very different picture emerged to that of the bright post-industrial future full of new opportunities. The survey data led inescapably to the conclusion that deindustrialization was producing a process of social polarization. At one pole were households that were comfortably placed with several of their members in work, while at the other extreme were households with no work. These latter households had the compensation of having plenty of time available to them, but this was scant consolation for the fact that they were unable to access opportunities to work (either in the formal labour market or informally). Thus society was gravitating towards a comfortable 'middle mass' of 'work-rich' households and an emerging 'underclass' of 'work-poor' households. Claire Wallace's complementary research among young people on Sheppey echoed this finding as the fortunes of 'swimmers' and 'sinkers' (1987: 140) diverged in a similar fashion.

Once discovered, this pattern made perfect if unpalatable sense. The logic of their respective situations meant that employment makes people better connected than their unemployed counterparts, who by contrast are isolated by their lack of connection. Opportunities for work in all its forms tend to gravitate towards people already occupied and to enhance their position, while marginality is also self-perpetuating. This phenomenon of community members being subjected to centripetal and centrifugal forces had been noted by previous community researchers (Crow 2002a: ch.4). Pahl's analysis went further by tracing how this outcome was reinforced through the operation of the welfare benefits system. His decision to focus attention on the household as the unit of analysis drove home how unemployment blighted the prospects not only of individuals but also of others with whom they live where there is relatively little to be gained financially by their being in work when the income from that work is deducted from their unemployed partner's welfare benefits. What mattered, in other words, was that the approach to economic activity adopted by a household needs to be viable as a household work strategy (Crow 1989). Pahl used this concept to show how households with multiple earners were prospering while those in which members were unemployed could find themselves constrained in terms of options available to them, and in the extreme trapped and reduced to following a dour, anxiety-ridden survival strategy.

Pahl's key theme in *Divisions of Labour* of changing patterns of work generating a relentless process of social polarization needed the survey of Sheppey households to discover it, but the exposition of the argument came through most forcefully using case studies of two households with contrasting fortunes. Pahl (1980) had already used this technique of comparing two households in an early and very provisional report on his fieldwork and these sketches of the Parsons and Simpson households are reproduced as an appendix to *Divisions of Labour*. By the end of the fieldwork, however, it was apparent to Pahl that the stories of two other couples, Linda and Jim and Beryl and George, functioned far better as illustrations of how social polarization played itself out at the household level. The chapter devoted to the two households comprises a full tenth of the whole book. In particular, Linda and Jim spoke for downwardly mobile people, and they did so in a way that echoed Pahl's higher-level theorizing. In one passage discussing access to job opportunities, he notes that 'Linda demonstrated her natural capacity as a sociologist by remarking aphoristically, "It's true what they say: it's not what you know now but who you know"' (1984: 298). Beryl and George merit some attention as representatives of the affluent, upwardly mobile members of the 'middle mass' leading comfortable, home-centred lives with all the benefits of steady and secure incomes, but it is Linda and Jim that have the lion's share of the chapter devoted to them. Even that could not do complete justice to their case since, in Pahl's opinion, 'in some ways they deserve a book to themselves' (1984: 304). The powerful nature of Linda and Jim's story is instantly apparent because it captures so effectively how much at variance their lives were from 'the so-called "informal" or "black" economy of popular misconception' (1984: 250). It is no surprise that Pahl continued visiting Linda and Jim for a further decade, for research purposes (Wilson and Pahl 1988) but also because of the depth of the personal connection that they achieved (Elliott and Lawrence, 2017).

Pahl's study warrants consideration as a modern classic (Crow and Ellis, 2017) because of the way that it addresses core social scientific concerns. The maxims drawn from Charles Wright Mills's (2000) manifesto for sociology about the discipline's capacity to illuminate the intersection of biography and history are so well known that Pahl did not need to reference his driving concern to 'focus on the connections between public issues and private troubles' (1984: 7). It is through the depth of attention given to Linda and Jim's story that Pahl's points hit home about downward mobility happening to people despite their best efforts to secure their economic position. It is a compelling story that provides a powerful indictment of popular perceptions of welfare 'scroungers' idling their time away supported by unemployment benefit, and of government policies founded on those perceptions. Durkheim may have been on methodologically sound ground when arguing that a single example does not prove a general rule, but Pahl was nevertheless correct in opting to use the case study to follow the extensive but dense statistical analysis of the survey data in a way that 'brought them alive' (1984: 277). The interpretation of the facts and figures derived from the survey about how households function was unarguable in the case made for needing to rethink the work done by individuals in different gender and social class positions, but there is also value in using the persuasive capacity of making an abstract idea embodied (Crow 2005: 45).

In a similar way, *Divisions of Labour* engaged readers by using Sheppey as a case study of how high-level processes like deindustrialization and globalization are expressed in a particular place. This is a strength of community studies generally, their capacity to make abstract notions more tangible, accessible and understandable (Crow 2000). Pahl's treatment of deindustrialization is a good example. The historical contextualization that he provides of Sheppey's development as an 'industrial island' serves to maximize the impact of the narrative that follows it of the loss of the dockyard as a major employer and the changed nature of industrial production in the factories and steelworks brought in to provide alternative employment. Woven into this narrative are further observations about how the world of work would have changed even without the closure of the Admiralty dockyard as the feminization of the workforce, the changing power of trade unions, and the modernization of employer attitudes and practices worked themselves through. These were national and global forces, but Pahl's analysis succeeds in portraying their local expression. The inclusion of ten contemporary photographs taken locally (1984: 182–3) aids readers' ability to grasp the realities of Sheppey and its people, to whom the book is dedicated.

Photographs thus added another dimension to Pahl's efforts to express 'the reality of ordinary people's lives' (1984: 8). They reflected his awareness that 'contemporary studies of local labour markets need to be seen in context' (1984: 155), because no two places are identical, and local distinctiveness is lost in macro-level analyses that overgeneralize. The behaviour of Sheppey people made more sense once the peculiarities of the place were appreciated, and so *Divisions of Labour* is at pains to convey the distinctiveness of the community's history, its housing and labour markets, and its culture. Pahl's longstanding interest in housing led him to attach particular significance to the fact that rates of owner-occupation were considerably higher on the island than the average for the UK overall (1984: 175–6). This was all the more remarkable given the fact that the wages paid to those islanders in work 'were not high' (1984: 171); owner-occupation did not necessarily signify affluent lifestyles. Pahl gained insights into the local labour market through visiting workplaces and speaking to employers; such elite interviews complemented conversations conducted with workers, and the book's narrative gives no sense of privileging accounts from either side of the employment relationship (although Pahl did incur a degree of displeasure locally by reporting some employers' opinions more frankly than may have been judicious).

The methodological message that comes through from the Sheppey study is the value of employing a wide range of different research methods in order to capture the multifaceted phenomenon that is 'community'. This research required contributions from numerous people with diverse but complementary skills. In addition to the specialist researchers brought in from Social and Community Planning Research to undertake the island-wide survey, Pahl also benefitted from the archival work undertaken by Nick Buck looking into the history of the dockyard, from research undertaken by Jane Dennett into the more recent history of industry, employment and housing development, and from the contributions of Claire Wallace to interviewing and to ethnographic and photographic elements of the project. Jim Styles also contributed to the photography, and the book also contains a map of the island. And at the heart of the varied activities, the 'large-scale, multi-faceted research project' (1984: 11) was Pahl himself, interviewing, conversing, observing, consulting records, keeping up with events through the local newspaper (which is quoted extensively in the book), and generally absorbing the various facets of community life on Sheppey. He remarked that, 'A perceptive observer visiting the Island would see and understand much by travelling about' (1984: 155), and Pahl was such an observer. He was also speaking from first-hand experience when noting that, 'Doing empirical research in sociology involves more cold waits in the rain, and more cups of tea or coffee when one really wants a solid meal, than is perhaps recognized' (1984: viii). He did, however, purchase a property in Sheerness so that his team had a base on Sheppey, and over a six-year period of fieldwork Pahl became much more than simply a visiting observer. He also did not cut his connections with Sheppey once the book was published, but continued to undertake research there and to keep up relationships, thereby highlighting that fieldwork connections can last for many years, sometimes decades (Crow 2012).

3.2 *The British on the Costa del Sol*

Karen O'Reilly's ethnographic research among expatriates in Spain led her to spend a much lengthier period in her fieldwork location than she had originally intended. On the basis of her own experience and that of others, she has commented that 'an ethnographer needs time' (2012: 16). A traditional model of ethnographic fieldwork involves researchers spending at least a year immersing themselves in the culture of the people whom they have chosen to investigate (Goffman 2002), but just as Pahl found himself going back to Sheppey more often than he had anticipated, the same is true for O'Reilly and her research location, Fuengirola. In her book, she reports that, 'I spent fifteen months in Spain with my family during 1993 and 1994 and have returned to the area many times over the years since then' (2000a: 10). Later on, this pattern of return visits was further extended in a process that she calls 'ethnographic returning' (O'Reilly 2012). She found, like Pahl, that the focus of the research evolved over the course of the time spent in the field, extending from the initial interest in how British migrants to Spain had managed that process to embrace much broader aspects of the practice of social life. Spain's British migrants were a focus of media attention, and so a public issue aspect to the research was present alongside the personal problems that people reported encountering. Indeed, individual stories of disappointment at the failure to realize the anticipated 'dream' lifestyle that migration had been expected to deliver were common enough to warrant, through the examination of myths, consideration of the puzzle of how people routinely come to be 'falsely conscious of their social positions' (Mills 2000: 5). Like Pahl, O'Reilly experienced one question leading to another which made it 'difficult to know when to stop' (2012: 532). Furthermore, ethnographers make the decision to leave the field influenced by many other factors besides the amount of material that they have collected, including ethical concerns about leaving study participants feeling that they have been exploited and then abandoned (Pole and Hillyard 2016: ch.6). Generating such disappointment is not only undesirable in itself, but also to be avoided because it makes things difficult for future researchers (Crow 2013; Hammersley and Atkinson 2007: 94–6).

O'Reilly was aware that community studies had been criticized for assuming an unproblematic relationship between communities and places. Focussing on a community of British migrants in Spain held great potential to explore this issue afresh. The book has the subtitle 'transnational identities and local communities'. Her research participants constituted a recognizable community in a particular locality, but they were quite different from the people who populated conventional community studies because they were still outsiders in many respects, such as not always being fluent in Spanish, the local language. In consequence they were not particularly well-integrated into the host society, and remained distinctly British. As a social group whose members did not readily blend in with their new surroundings, the British in Spain found their way regularly into the news, and not only because of the size of the migrant population (although that was in itself remarkable, running as it did into hundreds of thousands of people). The familiar community studies theme of 'us' and 'them' consciousness was prominent among research participants, but as migrants they could not construct a common identity around lifelong associations with a place or each other and so had to build a more complex narrative about what brought and held them together.

The situation was thus fertile ground for the study of how myths function in the construction of community identities. Myth and reality served as a useful analytical framework for exploring how there can be discrepancies between what migrants expect to find in their new environment and the situation that they encounter upon arrival. Pahl's early study of people moving to commuter villages taking with them idealized notions of what their new lives would be like, what he called 'villages in the mind' (Pahl 2005), was echoed in O'Reilly's transnational migrants not necessarily having realistic expectations about what awaited them. One of her participants complained of her compatriots that 'they all just want to live a fantasy life. It's not real!' (2000b: 243) In particular, many of them were not prepared for the social segregation that they would encounter. Thus O'Reilly reports that 'several men told me that they find it difficult to make friends in Spain' and adds that while women tended to be less forthcoming on the subject of isolation, she did nevertheless have conversations with them that conveyed 'that they sometimes feel terribly lonely and wish they could go home' (2000a: 82), having discovered that the downside of 'trading intimacy for liberty' (2000b) was a loss of depth to their friendships.

Immersion in ethnographic fieldwork has the great benefit of generating extensive field notes, and an extract from these allows the point to be illustrated far better than a quotation from an interview would:

> Later on that morning Joan and Beryl sat chatting over a cup of coffee. I heard Beryl say that she is much less bored here now that she has something to do with herself. She said that she used to get very bored and lonely, and people never really understood because they don't think you should. Joan seemed relieved to hear her say these things and started to tell how lonely and bored she gets, how she misses her family and how she feels she must not admit this to anyone. They said that people do not talk about things like

that here, they do not admit that they are lonely. ... They talked about how visitors are always jealous of them but don't realise that everything is not always perfect. (2000a: 83)

The key point here is that there can be significant discrepancies between people's 'public accounts' and their 'private accounts' (Cornwell 1984), and that unless a researcher can access the latter they are destined to remain in the restricted sphere of the public face that people present.

There are several good reasons why the public accounts presented by the British in Spain were positive. The active pursuit of migration to Spain represented an investment in the project, both financially and emotionally. The case for having made the move is something that they needed to be persuasive, and the people that they needed to convince that it was producing the desired outcomes were not only others but also themselves. There was therefore a readiness to subscribe to the belief that moving to Spain offers access to a desirable lifestyle; migrants to whom O'Reilly spoke 'seemed concerned to stress the benefits of life in Spain', and most 'wanted me to know that they had not made a mistake in moving to Spain' (2000a: 70, 13). The concept derived from Durkheim via Michael Crick of 'collective representations' is useful in conveying how a positive picture of the migrants' way of life was reproduced through reinforcement of the idea that it involves 'a healthy, happy lifestyle where elderly people are more active and more included than they would be back home' (O'Reilly 2000a: 2, 69). Thus alongside the compelling collective representation of Spain as somewhere that offered a good quality of life was a corresponding collective representation of Britain as problematic because of its weather and its social problems expressed in high rates of crime and the social marginalization of older people. Within this view of the world, the pull of Spain and the push from Britain combined to make migration a sensible course of action to take.

The ideal of community lies at the heart of this narrative about the case for moving to Spain. In contrast to the attractive, relaxed lifestyle in Spain that offered freedom, enjoyment and the opportunity to be yourself, migrants were 'continually constructing and reconstructing a negative image of Britain and a "bad Britain" discourse' that features, variously, 'routine; dullness; monotony; greyness; cold; no hope for the future; a miserable old age; misery; modern life; rushing around; no time for pleasure; crime; selfishness; lack of caring; loss of community; lack of trust;

poor health; poor education; and a poor welfare state' (2000a: 99). What is being expressed here is the 'loss of community' theme that has been a familiar feature of thinking about community change in a host of cases (Lee and Newby 1983: ch.4), but with the consolation that the lost social arrangements have been rediscovered in another context. Traditional values may have been subject to prolonged erosion in contemporary Britain, but longed-for community could be found instead in Spain. A British bar owner to whom O'Reilly spoke described his new home as 'like Britain was in the fifties – like turning the clocks back. Like the time that people knew their neighbours and cared about them, and you could go out and leave your door unlocked, and it was safe to walk the streets at night ... and families were close' (2000a: 115). The nostalgic tone of this description is instructive, revealing a longing for a past that is felt to be no longer available in Britain. It is more that Britain has changed than that the migrants have changed, although the idea that they have had to make no adjustment to their new environment is an oversimplification. Rather, it is that Spain had provided them with a setting in which they have been able to re-establish many valued patterns of community relationships, or at least to believe that they had done so.

Fieldwork encounters threw up much familiar community-related rhetoric. One British migrant claimed to be well-integrated with both Spanish and British neighbours, reporting it to be 'like a village here; one sneeze and we've all got a cold' (2000a: 101). Commitment to the move was reinforced by the absence of plans to return to Britain, and indeed antipathy to the idea, because of the 'unidealised view of home' (2000a: 98) that was held. Whereas other migrant groups such as Pakistanis in Britain have been found to operate with a 'myth of return' (Anwar 1985) that kept open the possibility of going back to a country of origin, O'Reilly interpreted the many statements along the lines of 'I've got no desire to go back there' to constitute a 'myth of (no) return' (2000a: 97, 96). The language of myth is appropriate here, because over time evidence emerged that returning to the UK was a common occurrence. First impressions of a permanently settled British community in Spain were misleading. During the initial phase of fieldwork O'Reilly was 'unaware of the various comings and goings in what turned out to be an important season for the community: the period of a huge temporary summer re-migration to the home country' (2000a: 13). As O'Reily's awareness of this pattern of people going back and forth grew, so she came to appreciate the heterogeneity of her study population. As a result, the simple distinction between tourists and settlers proved unworkable, and a more sophisticated typology evolved in which 'full residents', 'returning residents', 'seasonal visitors' and 'peripatetic visitors' (2000a: 52) were differentiated, all distinguishable from tourists. Several paragraph-long descriptions of individuals or couples are provided for each of the types, and this serves to further emphasize the heterogeneity of the British in Spain, with important differences being noted within as well as between the types.

The British on the Costa del Sol does not seek to cover everything. One of the six core topics of community research in the classic '*Middletown*' tradition, youth, would have been unproductive to pursue in Fuengirola, because teenagers are uncommon among the British in Spain. Given that people over the age of fifty are a prominent part of the migrant population, there would have been plenty of reasons to justify a focus on retirement migration, as other researchers have done (Ahmed 2015; King, Warnes and Williams 2000; Oliver 2008). Previous research into retirement migration in the UK such as that by Valerie Karn (1977) was clearly being superseded by the opening up of opportunities for international mobility, and O'Reilly's findings do much to reveal the extent of this change, but she is at pains to confront 'the assumption that the British in Spain are mainly elderly and retired' (2000a: 9). Among the 259 people living in and around Fuengirola from whom she collected data, more than three-fifths were under the age of sixty, and although this was not a representative sample of British people living in Spain, it did enough to convey that there are 'large numbers of migrants who do not fit neatly into typologies or stereotypes formed by other authors and commentators' (2000a: 60). Not only was there variation in the ages at which people migrated, there was also diversity introduced by the presence of opportunities to combine drawing a pension with undertaking different kinds of work. Ostensibly retired people were to be found among those 'working informally ... involved in all sorts of activities from home maintenance, decorating and ironing, to taxying, pool maintenance and car mechanics' (2000a: 122). This finding would not necessarily have emerged had the study adopted a more conventional focus and categorization.

O'Reilly's primary concern was not with numerical data. The approach that she adopted of participant observation was justified by her belief that 'people and actions cannot simply be observed, logged and counted but require interpretation, understanding and empathy' (2000a: 10).

Suspicions about the problematic status of statistics on migration were soon confirmed. Statistical data on British migrants to Spain were sparse, and those that were available were prone to significant variation; some were little better than educated guesswork. The reasons for this were not hard to find. Not only was it the case that people who settled permanently were just one of several types of migrants alongside others who travelled back and forth between Spain and the UK, it was also apparent that by no means all migrants had gone through the formalities of acquiring appropriate legal documentation. In some quarters it had the reputation of being 'an expensive, time-consuming and bureaucratic nightmare'. British migration to Spain is both fluid and quite often not recorded officially and as a result is 'very difficult to quantify' (2000a: 46, 41). A further character of the migrant population that presents a challenge to attempts to quantify its dimensions relates to the fact that 'for the British themselves the identity as permanent or temporary migrant does not always seem to depend on clear, objective criteria'. Some participants' narratives suggested that an important part of migrants' expectations being fulfilled could be expressed by reference to involvement in an active social life, and O'Reilly found there to be 'numerous British-run clubs and social groups' (2000a: 104, 120). It would have been possible for her to follow Robert Putnam's (2000) influential methodological strategy of taking voluntary organization membership as a quantitative indicator of social capital, but she did not. The community networks that have grown up among the British migrants are characterized by informality, and that makes participation in them hard to measure. Her emphasis on 'the informal construction of social and community life' (2000a: 124), as well as her discussion of how such informality shades into illegality (2000b: 237), highlights parallels between these social networks of exchange and the informal economy studied by researchers like Pahl.

The penultimate chapter in O'Reilly's book is entitled 'The construction of community'. The way in which the individuals being studied constitute a 'community' is instructive because the people involved are far from static; they 'are changing all the time'. Put another way, it is a community whose members' mobility makes it vulnerable to 'the threat of transience' (2000a: 133, 132). The question of what members of a community have in common is raised particularly starkly in this case. Of the three possible answers of place, interests and identity delineated by Peter Willmott (1986), it is shared identity that comes out most strongly in the analysis.

Spain in general and the Costa del Sol in particular are necessarily reference points in the constructed community, but this is not a population
with rootedness in the place over generations. Shared interests feature in
people's accounts of how exchange and reciprocity are integral to community members' lives, but O'Reilly's argument is that such exchanges are
more important for their symbolic value than they are for their monetary
value. What drives the making of this community is a shared commitment to particular values, or at least the quest to achieve them. Among
these values, egalitarianism featured prominently, with the claim asserted
frequently that past lives in Britain had no bearing on a person's status
in Spain. People were said to be accepted as equals, provided that they
showed commitment to the community's slow pace of life, its informality
and its endorsement of responsibility, caring and supportiveness; these are
all familiar elements of thinking about 'community', and it is unsurprising
to find them deployed in this context.

It is also unsurprising to find the reality not always living up to these
ideals. In this community, as in many others, higher status was accorded
to people who had lived there longer. Newcomers were necessarily at a
disadvantage compared to those who 'have more to bring to the exchange
in the way of knowledge, contacts and goods.... Knowledge of the area, of
the pitfalls of settling there, of laws and regulations, and of where to go or
who to ask to get what, is highly valued.' O'Reilly also found 'a definite class
divide' (2000a: 127, 131) present in people's patterns of sociability, while
reference to shared Britishness did not always transcend Scots, Welsh,
English and Irish backgrounds. Even more importantly, there were marked
discrepancies between claims to involvement with the host society and
the realities of the largely separate lives led by many Britons in Spain.
Migrants were 'constructing an isolated community yet pretending that
they were integrated ... acting ethnically but denying that' (2000a: 153).
Observing that people say one thing but do something quite different is
of course a social science commonplace, and so the discovery of a 'gloss
of commonality' is at one level unremarkable. Its wider significance is
twofold. Methodologically it means that researchers face the challenge of
getting beyond the public face that people present, to penetrate the realm
of 'private discourse' and to attach credibility to what is said privately,
even if the participant goes on to 'vehemently deny it in public' (2000a:
130, 134). The second point is theoretical. O'Reilly draws on the work of
Cohen (1985) to approach community's appeal as a route through which

individuals can reinforce their sense of self. Community is symbolically important, providing individuals with a sense of who they are and how they are different from other people whose lives lie beyond the boundaries of the familiar way of life of fellow community members. O'Reilly's participant who recounted her search for 'like-minded people' (2000b: 234) spoke unwittingly for many others beside herself.

3.3 The Other Side of Middletown

Community studies can be produced by lone scholars or by teams. O'Reilly's research was undertaken single-handedly for her PhD, and is a testament to what can be achieved in that format. Diverse studies have come out of individuals' doctoral theses including Allan (1979), Bell (1994), Benson (2011), Brent (2009), Charlesworth (2000), Cornwell (1984), Devine (1992), Eade (1989), Farrar (2002), Foster (1990), Frankenberg (1990), Gallaher (1961), Littlejohn (1963), Lummis (1985), Mah (2012), Pahl (1965), Pryce (1979), Rapport (1993), Roberts (1993), Rosenlund (2009), Scheper-Hughes (2001), Shaw (1988), Tunstall (1969) and Wight (1993). *Divisions of Labour*, although single-authored, is by contrast an example of what can be achieved by a research team. The third exemplar of community studies that this chapter focuses on is also the product of teamwork, but teamwork of a different kind that requires the active involvement of members of the community as participants in a collaborative project. *The Other Side of Middletown* is a remarkable book in several respects. First, it offers proof positive that collaborative ethnography can be successful; at the time of its publication, this case still needed to be made (Lassiter 2005). Secondly, it demonstrates that a large group of collaborators who from the outside might look too heterogeneous to work together effectively can function not only productively but also efficiently; the book's publication date of 2004 makes the reader double check the Introduction's opening sentence which reports that the project began only in January of the previous year, 2003 (Lassiter et al. 2004: 1). Thirdly, it stands as confirmation of the justification for restudies, making the case that there is plenty to be discovered by going back; even in a community with such a long and celebrated history of being researched as Muncie (Caccamo 2000), there are new sides to local social life yet to be uncovered, or 'missing pieces' of puzzles to be located (Lassiter 2012).

Awareness of the fact that there was an unrecorded side of the city's story featured in the gestation of the project. Despite the local African

American population constituting a significant element of the city's composition, they had surprisingly been virtually invisible in the various research reports on Muncie from the original *Middletown* studies of the Lynds onwards. There was thus a record to be put straight and justice to be done for a group that, in the face of this track record of academic neglect, might understandably have been suspicious of researchers' intentions. Researchers who use collaborative methods are able to offer some reassurance in situations where trust has to be established, and Lassiter and his academic colleagues could make a convincing pitch that involvement of community members would proceed according to 'a collaborative vision for the ethnography's goals and purposes' (Lassiter 2005: xi). Emphasis was placed on the responsibility of people involved to be respectful and accountable, and to see the project through. The project team comprised the collaborative ethnographer Lassiter, the local civil rights activist Hurley Goodall and his wife Fredine, the folklorist and ethnographer Elizabeth Campbell, the graduate assistant Michelle Johnson, fourteen undergraduate student researchers (comprising both black and white students) studying a range of disciplines, twelve community 'advisors', a further fifty-eight contributors from Muncie's African American community, along with numerous others in supporting and facilitative roles who are acknowledged in the book's Introduction. Lassiter describes the students' achievement of collecting over 150 hours of recorded material from a total of more than 60 people in the space of four months as 'an amazing feat' (Lassiter et al. 2004: 13), not only because of the amount of data amassed but also because the process was managed within the ethos of the collaborative approach.

The reported rapidity with which the project was completed is potentially misleading. This is not to take anything away from the intensity with which the various people involved worked to collect, analyse, discuss and write up material on the same six themes that had been the focus of the Lynds' original reports. It is important to note, however, that the project team assembled at the beginning of 2003 were not starting from scratch: they were able to draw extensively on two things, a sizeable grant from the Virginia Ball Center (Campbell and Lassiter 2014: 15–19), and local knowledge that was already available. Pivotal in this latter respect was the fact that Hurley Goodall's career as a community activist had led him to collect 'community photographs, church histories, newspaper clippings, and individual narratives for well over three decades'. It also located him and Fredine at the heart of the city's community, ideally placed to 'spread the word throughout Muncie' (2004: 3, 7). Lassiter and Campbell's collaboration with the Goodalls had been developing around other activities for several years by the time that *The Other Side of Middletown* project took shape, and without this foundation it is doubtful that the positive working relationships that characterized the project would have emerged quite as readily. Nevertheless, projects can develop momentum to carry them along at speed, and the students' field notes conveyed how quickly immersion in a community can be achieved. Sarah Bricker, working on the 'using leisure' theme, attended a church service in only the second month of the project and noted being reassured by just how many of the congregation she recognized and who welcomed her; as her fieldnotes recorded, 'Everyone waved or said hello.' Johnson's observation in her role of graduate assistant that 'collaboration did not happen overnight. ... It progressed slowly during the first three to four weeks of the project' (2004: 14, 274) gives an indication of the tight schedule that the participants were on; year-long fieldwork was an unaffordable luxury in a semester-long project.

Among those working on the project, the students in particular found themselves on a steep learning curve. Of the fourteen undergraduates, eight had either anthropology or sociology as part of their degree, but others came from subjects at greater remove from the community studies tradition, such as journalism, English, philosophy and telecommunications. Whatever their disciplinary background, they all had to realize that while collaborating on a project with other students can be hard, collaborating with members of a community who are outside of academia has the potential to take challenges to another level. The commitment made to 'establish good rapport with the community so that future collaborative studies can be undertaken' includes collaborative writing, so that the chapters produced by the six groups allocated to produce accounts of work, home, youth, leisure, religion and community action went through many iterations and much scrutiny. Comments from community advisers on drafts produced by students could on occasion be expressed robustly, although in general they were typically more hesitant than the critique given by Lassiter, Campbell, Johnson and another academic, Robert Nowatzki, which made some of the students 'angry and hurt' about how far short of publishable standard their drafts had been adjudged, including by the eventual publisher. Johnson uses the word 'negotiation' (2004: 20, 18, 276) to describe the process of repeated redrafting following comments. This conveys that there are several different points of view to be accommodated in collaborative ethnography.

The situation in which researchers confront competing and possibly conflicting agendas and sets of expectations about the outcomes of their efforts is not new. Robert Lynd's 1939 book *Knowledge for What?* was inevitably influenced by his experience of years of researching 'Middletown', and his conclusion about the need to work according to 'the spirit of science' reflected the emphasis that he placed on researchers being prepared to pose difficult questions and pursue 'dangerous hypotheses'. As an illustration he gave the example of social class inequalities, and found the work of his contemporaries wanting: 'Current social science plays down the omnipresent fact of class antagonisms and conflicts in the living all about us' (1939: 249, 227). *Middletown in Transition* had broached the subject of social class much more explicitly than the Lynds had done in the original *Middletown*, and in the process alienated some readers. For the authors of *The Other Side of Middletown*, the issues of race and racism were the central ones that had to be confronted; these also are not comfortable topics. The research team were mindful of the need to avoid reproduction and reinforcement of popular stereotypes of African Americans. This issue came up when the group allocated the topic of the home discovered that they had unintentionally given misleading impressions about the prevalence of households headed by single parents. Having been prompted by community advisers to solicit the stories of lone mothers, who opened up opportunities to interview other lone parents, some advisers then 'encouraged the students to focus, as well, on dual-parent homes lest the students stereotype the community in their writings and forego the actual diversity of families'. The section of the book that presents the stories of single parents prefaces these with the comment that 'strong families do not necessarily consist of two parents and a certain number of children' (Lassiter et al. 2004: 10, 105). In addition, a valuable lesson had been learned about the risk of 'snowball' sampling, leading to an overconcentration on one particular part of a community.

Racism as a theme runs strongly through the other five topics considered in the book as well as making a home. It is there in accounts of getting a living, training the young, using leisure, engaging in religious practices and engaging in community activities. This demonstrates the capacity of the community study approach to bring out the connectedness of different aspects of people's everyday life, for example the importance of social networks for the way in which the range of people that someone knows affects their chances of getting a job. With black people having fewer personal connections than white people to those in positions to recruit employees, Hurley Goodall opined that they 'have to jump twice as high to even get the opportunity because there is no relationship between our community and the people running these institutions. That makes it doubly hard' (2004: 237). Chapter 2 describes Muncie as 'a city apart' and charts the history of the black community's experience of exclusion, including segregation into distinct neighbourhoods. For the Lynds, writing in the 1930s, African Americans were the city's 'most marginal population' (1937: 465), and the map inside the book's front and back covers shows the geographical expression of this. The continuing separateness of the black community as a particular 'place on the ground' is expressed in statistics relating to the two predominantly black neighbourhoods of Whitely and Industry, which were respectively 71 per cent and 84 per cent African American in their composition (2004: 232, 233). Spatial separation in housing feeds in to other forms of apartness, as Hurley Goodall observes, 'Community here in Muncie consists of two totally different communities. One white, with distinct geographic, economic, and religious boundaries; and another black, with the same structures that meet and interact when mutual survival requires it' (2004: 232). Physical separateness inevitably shapes people's home life, their education, their work, their religious association, their leisure and their involvement in community activities.

The point about the connectedness of the various elements of a community is a universal one. For a minority community, a further observation can be made about how the specifics of their situation are not equally appreciated. Hurley Goodall frames this issue by asking, 'Why does Middletown's African-American population have such an obsession with racism in Middletown? Because black people will talk to you about it just about anytime you want to talk to them about it. The white community is just the opposite. They have so much difficulty admitting racism is a serious problem in the community' (2004: 233–4). Part of the answer to this question is that white people can be unaware of the phenomenon, or at least be disengaged from it, in a way that black people cannot be because it is a different experience to be on the receiving end of racism, as many of the personal narratives contained in the book bear out. A further point is the astute observation of one of the white students on the project, Eric Efaw, who noted, 'As many of my advisors have expressed to me, minorities have to interact with the Euro-American majority community on a daily basis, but whites are able to more or less isolate themselves from other ethnicities if they so choose' (2004: 257). He went on to comment that understanding of other cultures requires people to be prepared to put themselves in situations where they might feel out of place. He and the other students on the project had been required to do this, most obviously in the case of the white students who were going into the black community, but also for the black students whose experiences of everyday racism sometimes differed from those told to them by the consultants, particularly those narratives that related to earlier periods of history when discrimination included forms that have in the meantime been outlawed.

No claims are made for *The Other Side of Middletown* to be definitive in what it says about Muncie. One of the consequences of the pace at which the project had to be conducted is that the members of the city's African American community who were involved are not representative of the wider population; they were 'primarily, although not exclusively, ... older (often retired) middle-class collaborators (who had the time to work intensively with us within this short time-frame)' (2004: 22). In this sense the book marks the beginning of a new conversation which others may join and add different dimensions of experience through future projects. Any such future conversations will be informed by what the project has revealed about typicality. The omission of Muncie's African American inhabitants from previous '*Middletown*' studies had come about partly because researchers in pursuit of a 'typical' community had ended up working with notions of the average American that screened out differ-ence and diversity (Igo 2007). The key lesson here is that the heterogeneity of populations can be overlooked by methods that deal with averages and representativeness, and by concepts of 'community' that focus only on commonalities. In the process the object under investigation is reduced to a misleadingly idealized construction.

Sarah Igo's characterization of Lynds' study as the work of 'social scien-tific amateurs' (2007: 31) may be somewhat harsh, but her more general point about the need to be mindful of how research findings will be received and used is undoubtedly correct: presentation matters for the messages that audiences take away with them.

The authors of *The Other Side of Middletown* wanted to present an authentic and engaging portrayal of Muncie's African Americans that they had co-operated in making and in which they would recognize themselves.

The project had set out 'to fully embrace the experiences of our consultants, their memories, and their stories' (Lassiter et al. 2004: 21), and the feel of the place and its people is conveyed effectively through collaborators' contributions that are extensively reproduced. People's educational histories, accounts of working careers, stories of making family life in the home, and narratives of engagement in religious and leisure activities and community politics form the core of the book. The details of these stories and the way in which they are expressed are compelling, as in Dolores Rhinehart's conviction expressed in the discussion of getting a living about the importance of budgeting on a low income: 'It's not what you make, it's what you do with what you make' (2004: 95). Supplementing the text are thirty-six photographs taken by one of the students, Danny Gawlowski (whose degree included photojournalism), and a further fourteen historical photographs. Gawlowski took many more photographs than were finally selected for inclusion, because the images required changed on each occasion that the text was rewritten. The ethnographic method of participant observation is more adequately reported where textual description is supplemented by images, but the observations made by the students as participants continued to expand in line with their attendance at the 'numerous family gatherings, school meetings, sporting events, church services, political rallies' (2004: 13) to which they found themselves invited. As a result, the photographer was left feeling that his work could have gone on indefinitely, but there is no question that the photographs add a valuable dimension to the book.

Lassiter suggests that the term 'participant observation' does not fully capture the nature of the fieldwork undertaken by the students, arguing that there was also a process of 'observant participation' going on. Students were encouraged 'to observe their own participation just as closely as they were observing others', and to include in their field notes a record of how their understanding evolved as their experience of being in the field proceeded. Research changes the researcher. The student authors of the 'training the young' chapter recorded how they had grown in confidence after only a short while: 'We felt comfortable now, showing up at events as outsiders and talking to strangers, trying to find out the stories that belonged to these people and places.' On occasion the researchers had to deal with potentially stereotyping representations of the African American community, that they were careful to report had been presented to them rather than being their own observations, such as 'Selling drugs has become the preferred way to make a living for some young people, according to some of our consultants' (2004: 94, 152). The fact that the project was able to broach such social problems and arrive at accounts of them that were acceptable to everyone involved stands as evidence of what collaborative working can achieve. For Lassiter, the book reflects the trend in the field of community research whereby 'both community study scholars and the people with whom we work are more regularly looking to collaborative research frameworks to close the gap between academically situated and community-based discourse'. The case for this approach is not only that the resultant research outputs have more resonance with and acceptability to community members, but also that it can contribute to making a difference in the world through the action that it prompts: 'An engaged social science can work toward change' (2012: 428, 435), and collaborative ethnography is one way of pursuing that agenda. In the process the rationales available for undertaking a community study are added to, and these rationales are the subject of the next chapter.

4 Worthwhileness

A researcher's decision to undertake a community study may be based on a variety of reasons. In the three exemplars discussed in the preceding chapter it is possible to identify quite a few of these potential groundings. Lassiter and his team were interested in giving voice to a community whose members had previously been unacknowledged, as a way of pursuing an agenda of change. Pahl's reasons for embarking on his study were less predetermined in what started out as a more open-ended project exploring the changing nature of work, but by the end of the book he had certainly given voice to Linda and Jim and people like them whose experience of downward social mobility bore little resemblance to popular stereotypes. In this way it could be regarded as putting into practice Elias's (1978: ch.2) description of sociologists as destroyers of myths. O'Reilly's investigation also engaged with mythology as it related to the idealization of community by her participants, but there is more of a sense in her work of understanding how myths contribute to the smooth operation of everyday life as people pursue the ideal of community as a type of quest (Thorns 1976). Her rationale is therefore that of exploratory social science, and this fits with her understanding that ethnographers do not set out to test theories but to make sense of both strange and ordinary phenomena that capture the researcher's imagination as interesting, including things that arise serendipitously. These three studies do not exhaust the range of rationales for community studies research, but they do show that several are available to researchers.

The underpinning rationale of a community study is a matter of interest to others besides researchers. The collaborative approach adopted in *The Other Side of Middletown* is based on the recognition that community members play an integral role in community research, since it could not proceed without them. This may lead to an instrumental focus on the potential usefulness of research to community members. Oscar Lewis recalled how at a meeting convened as part of his restudy of Tepoztlán in

Mexico, 'One dignified, elderly Tepoztecan rose and said, "Many people have come here to study us, but not one of them has helped us"' (1963: xv). The record of the benefits brought by being researched will be less bleak elsewhere, but the point remains salutary, that it is reasonable for community members to question why research that does not benefit them should proceed. Indeed, there are legitimate concerns that research could even be harmful to community members, for example through damage to individual or collective reputations, and cases of such adverse effects have contributed to the tightening of ethical regulation in recent decades. Funders of research will also be interested in ethical scrutiny of proposed projects that they are being asked to support. Such considerations extend beyond the avoidance of research participants suffering harm to include a desire to screen out projects that are adjudged a waste of participants' time or of funders' money. Research needs to have a point to be justified, and it also needs to be sufficiently rigorous and authentic to be taken seriously by its various intended audiences.

The rationale for doing community studies is that such research is useful through resulting in some practical beneficial outcome, or interesting for how it advances social scientific knowledge, and ideally both. There are numerous examples of community studies that have a practical rationale that in addition produce interesting findings and others that are framed primarily by social scientific puzzles that also have practical outcomes. Primarily useful research frequently arises out of concern with a social problem, of which there are many that have a community dimension, including education, housing, health, crime and welfare. This list is not identical with what the Lynds identified as the six 'main trunk activities' (1929: 5) by which life in *Middletown* (and elsewhere) might be analysed. The themes of work, home and education can readily be associated respectively with problems of unemployment and discrimination in the labour market, family poverty and insecure housing, or underachievement and bullying, but a research agenda driven by social problems would not necessarily direct as much attention to leisure, religion and community action. The distinction between social problems and sociological problems is helpful here, because it allows space to make the case for both types of research, so that investigators can produce monographs on *Redundancy and Recession* (Harris 1987) and also on *The Welsh In Patagonia* (Williams 1991). The title of the former flags up its relevance to the social problem of unemployment, while the latter is more in the tradition of titles indicating a study of people in a place, and by these different routes both studies have useful and interesting things to say.

4.1 Useful and interesting research

Community studies contribute to knowledge of social problems by locating them in context, and better understanding is a necessary (but not a sufficient) condition for moving towards solutions to these problems. Unemployment provides a good example. Coincidentally, the point is made in each of the three exemplars considered in the previous chapter, including by Pahl's participant Linda, that an individual's access to job opportunities is mediated by the people known to them, and Linda's insight was echoed by Daniel Wight's Scottish participants: 'It's no' *what* ye ken, it's *who* ye ken' (1993: 93, emphases in original). Community studies highlight the variable connectedness of individuals, and this insight was developed by Chris Harris (1987) and his colleagues, exploring how the dense connections characteristic of occupational communities built around a dominant local employer can have the effect of limiting the flow of information about job opportunities elsewhere. When large-scale employers run down their operations, people made redundant are better placed to find alternative employment if they have connections beyond their immediate community, however tenuous these may be. In the language of social network analysis, this demonstrates 'the strength of weak ties' (Granovetter 1973) for those who have them; by contrast, people embedded in dense but geographically restricted networks of kinship, friendship and local religious, political and leisure-time associations are more constrained. The problem arises not only because it is the case that 'people's social fields are generally local' but also because 'attachment with locality is likely to increase with age' (Harris 1987: 101), so that out-migration is more typically associated with the young, while redundancy among older and less geographically mobile workers poses particularly acute challenges.

Dense social networks may be regarded as problematic to the extent that they discourage outward mobility, but they should not be cast as less valuable than weak ties crossing community boundaries that are drawn upon only periodically. It was a principal finding of Young and Willmott's (1957) study of East London that people who were moved to improved housing beyond the locality found that this came at the cost of lost community support, and this theme has been echoed many times subsequently. Referring to the Netherlands cities of Amsterdam and Rotterdam, Talja Blokland and Flotis Noordhoff argue that, 'Everyday survival in poor urban communities frequently depends on close interaction with kin and friends in similar situations' (2008: 108), and that urban redevelopment that threatens these ties is at best a mixed blessing. These port cities have seen transformations of their employment bases, but patterns of community support and solidarity built up around local industries can survive the subsequent decline of those industries. Historical legacies endure, even as 'neighbourhood and work have grown apart' (Blokland 2003: 112). The same has been reported for London's East End (Foster 1999), areas formerly associated with mining (Warwick and Littlejohn 1992; Wight 1993), car production (Bryson and Winter 1999) and deindustrialization generally (Mah 2012; Pappas 1989); all echo Pahl's (1984) theme of the dockyard's influences on Sheppey long outlasting its closure.

Social problems can accompany not only the contraction of local employment but also its expansion. In *The Social Impact of Oil*, Robert Moore explored the consequences for the fishing town of Peterhead of the arrival in the 1970s of industries associated with the exploitation of North Sea oil. He found no shortage of expectations among local people that the development would bring a range of social problems but concluded that in practice the impact could be summarized as 'higher house prices, some unsightly camps and a few additional prostitutes'. Other problems that developed in the period such as 'increased teenage drinking [and] marital breakdown' were attributable to broader social change, and Moore commented that, 'The inhabitants of Peterhead are good enough sociologists not to call these simply "the effects of oil."' He also argued that his research revealed the presence of popular misconceptions of community which make evaluation of change difficult. He found many Peterheadians adhered to an image of the town as 'small, self-contained, relatively homogeneous with a shared oral history and a common culture' (1982: 151, 108, 79), but this idea of community autonomy flew in the face of its integration into the wider society, while images of togetherness were belied by the presence of hierarchical social distinctions and a long history of out-migration. Moore's initial focus on the disruptive effects of the arrival of a new industry expanded to encompass the broader issue of how people have a capacity to romanticize how their communities had been prior to recent changes, and in doing so he had much in common with Stacey's (1960) experience of studying of Banbury and George Giarchi's

(1984) of studying Dunoon following the arrival of new industries. Moore also shared with Stacey the experience of writing a book that did not please everyone locally, something Moore had also encountered previously in Sparkbrook in his work with Rex.

A third example of a study of a social problem leading on to the re-examination of broader social scientific themes is provided by informal care and social support. Preparedness of neighbours, friends and kin beyond households to contribute to a person's welfare is central to 'community'; interest in the topic reflects ongoing concerns about its perceived decline and the resultant social isolation of groups such as older people. Nickie Charles and her colleagues' (2008) restudy of Swansea was particularly well-placed to shed light on this issue because comparisons could be made with Rosser and Harris's research in the city four decades previously. The broad conclusion was that there has been a degree of change in perceptions of preparedness to provide mutual aid, but that strong continuities were also present, and the thesis of community involvement giving way to individualized lifestyles was not confirmed. People helping each other in community contexts still matters. The research design's sophistication allowed Charles and her colleagues to do better than paint a misleadingly uniform picture. Data collected from four contrasting areas of the city enabled more nuanced arguments to be developed, for example that middle-class areas had looser and more open social networks compared to the more closed character of mutual support found in working-class areas and also among the city's Bangladeshi-origin ethnic minority. The study also highlights the importance of gender: 'It is largely women's networks which hold families and communities together' (2008: 209); conversely it is among men that cases of social isolation are more likely to be found. These findings are remarkably in line with those of Fred St Leger and Norman Gillespie (1991) who explored similar issues in three communities in Belfast. Community relationships have a gendered character, and overly general language about 'communities' may lead to this being overlooked.

Practical interest in arrangements that promote informal care and social support is connected to questions about the research methods and concepts used to understand these phenomena. Charles and her colleagues make the point that working with research participants to complete network diagrams allowed them to recognize the extent to which choice is exercised in the construction of contemporary support networks. Kinship featured prominently, especially in the more working-class neighbour-hoods, but friends were subject to greater discretion, with a tendency to include those people judged to be 'like family', understood as being reli-able in times of crisis. Personal networks were not restricted to people liv-ing in the same neighbourhood, and not all of a person's neighbours were part of their 'personal communities' (2008: 210, 211). This concept has been used in other studies. For Chris Phillipson and his colleagues, who used personal network diagrams to investigate the changing position of older people, personal communities reflect people's greater choice about those with whom connections are cultivated. One of their principal findings was that 'friendships of different kinds ... have become of greater significance', and this had made their community horizons less geographically bound. This finding mattered particularly in their Bethnal Green fieldwork site, where white and Bengali residents could be neighbours yet have only shal-low contact with each other, coexisting as separate, 'encapsulated' (2001: 132, 255) communities.

4.2 Interesting and useful research

Many other instances of policy-relevant research producing not only prac-tical, useful findings but also interesting advances in the methodological and conceptual approaches adopted by social scientists could be given. For example, criminological research also problematizes the notion of communities as spatially bounded entities characterized by integrated, mutually supportive populations (Foster 1990; Mooney and Neal 2009; Sparks, Girling and Loader 1999). In the extreme case of hackers in cyber-space, they can be conceived of as 'a community even when the links between the members of the community are as free of physical space as it is possible to be' (Jordan 2002: 252). The study in its community context of any number of topics (such as crime, care, health, disability, education, unemployment, ethnicity, housing or regeneration) revisits the issue that exercised an earlier generation of critics of community studies for whom Pahl (1968) spoke through his critique of geographical determinism: where a person lives does not dictate how they live. It is instructive that Pahl con-tinued to grapple with this problem throughout his career, well beyond his time on Sheppey. His final book, co-written with Liz Spencer (Spencer and Pahl 2006), drew on the idea of personal communities comprised of friendships that modern conditions of geographical mobility and mobile communications have allowed to be freed from the constraints of residential proximity. Friends do not have to be local.

Various threads have fed into the related notions of personal communities and communities of choice. These include research involving lesbian and gay respondents who have found themselves excluded from conventional understandings of community yet wanting to assert the supportive, affirming, community-like character of their networks (Weeks, Heaphy and Donovan 2001). Spencer and Pahl's motivation to research friendship was not primarily one of seeking to better understand a social problem, as friendship in itself is a social good, but the results of the study turned out to be useful as well as interesting. This was in much the same way that the Sheppey project was curiosity-driven but nevertheless allowed Pahl to contribute to a book with the policy-relevant title *Is It Worth Working?* (Bryson and McKay 1994). Thus the finding that people whose friendships were more geographically dispersed were not necessarily 'more isolated', nor more vulnerable to having 'fewer intimate or supportive relationships' was instructive, and taken further by the observation that the personal communities considered most robust 'usually contain local as well as dispersed sources of sociability and support' (Spencer and Pahl 2006: 195, 206). The ideal is to have both local and non-local network members.

Barry Wellman's writings have done much to popularize the idea of personal communities. His writing on social networks mediated via the internet builds on his earlier investigations into how people's social lives were being freed from dependence on neighbourhoods through the development of pre-internet technologies (such as cars and telephones). The residents of the East York area of Toronto were found to have thriving patterns of sociability and reciprocity, just not necessarily with each other. People's ties were no longer 'organised into densely knit, tightly bounded solidarities' (1979: 1206) within the confines of neighbourhoods, from which they had been liberated by active engagement with the opportunities opening up to them. Internet communities have made it possible to explore the issue of whether people can use virtual connection to leave further behind place-based connectedness, as some speculative narratives have suggested might be the case. The situation in practice is less dramatic, Wellman concludes: 'Despite the dazzling portrayals of virtual worlds whose denizens only meet online, in reality, most ties combine in-person with computer-mediated contact' (1999a: xx). The coming of the internet has not fundamentally changed the pattern whereby connections between people are made using other media in between episodes of face-to-face interaction. Nor, it seems, is the content of interactions between people all that different even in more exclusively internet based communities whose members do not meet in the same physical space. The exchange of information may figure more prominently in internet communities as a proportion of what happens, but 'companionship, emotional support, services, and a sense of belonging are abundant in cyberspace' (Wellman and Gulia 1999: 353). With reference back to the discussion about the policy-relevant research on the caring capacities of communities, and the sources of personal well-being, this finding indicates that research into internet communities has useful applications as well as being interesting in and of itself.

Related research by Rich Ling into mobile communication can be used to make similar points about social research not needing to be designed to address social problems in order to be useful. The spread of mobile phones has meant that small groups of friends are 'contacting one another with more frequency and the family is better able to monitor one another's needs. We are in continual, if brief and topical contact' (2008: 186). Ling's interpretation of these developments is that they do not fit neatly into classical sociological models of the transition from Tönnies's *gemeinschaft* to *gesellschaft*, or Durkheim's mechanical-to-organic solidarity, and he turns instead to ideas developed by Erving Goffman about the contribution of everyday ritual to social cohesion. Frequent contact between friends and family members by mobile phone conversations and texting 'has resulted in tighter integration of the group', and the possibility of such connections at any time has further reinforced this. Moreover, Ling argues, it has taken only a very short period of time for this medium of communication to have become not only normalized but for the shift to be so commonplace as to be unrecognized; mobile communication has become 'in the literal sense, not remarkable' (2008: 173). This observation is pertinent to the question of how best to research virtual communities. In contrast to Wellman's (1999b) reliance on survey techniques to explore the strong ties in the ego-centred networks that make up personal communities of which people were aware, Ling's approach involved both quantitative and qualitative elements including ethnographic observations and '"gonzo" experiments' (2008: 20) to get at unrecorded norms of behaviour. His study included field notes about strangers' use of mobile phones in public places and their responses when Ling placed himself in unusually close physical proximity to them. This is useful knowledge in the same way that Goffman's analysis of the need to maintain and repair civility in public encounters is good to know.

Other research into virtual communities has drawn on the idea of 'imagined communities', which Benedict Anderson (1991) developed to analyse nationalism (see Blackshaw 2010: 118–24). This idea does not fit readily into the community studies genre of empirical research, however, since Anderson's purpose was to explore people's preparedness to identify with an abstract collectivity whose members could not possibly have face-to-face connections, except with a very small minority. As Vered Amit notes, 'Anderson's work deliberately decoupled the idea of community from an actual base of interaction' (2002: 6), and Anderson is less concerned with communities being either genuine or false than with 'the style in which they are imagined' (Anderson 1991: 6). However, Anderson's concept does remind us that communities are social constructions, and the role of imagination in community construction deserves attention. It is an element in Glyn Williams's (1991) *The Welsh In Patagonia*, in which the story of the settlement founded in a part of Argentina by Welsh-speaking immigrants in the mid-nineteenth century and its development as an ethnic community is told. Williams's justification of his research 'in the name of knowledge' (1991: x) is offered because more practical ration-ales for such historical research may not be ready to hand in the field, but there are grounds for treating this study as both interesting and useful. Fieldwork requiring fluency in three languages that took over a decade and involved archival research, the study of diaries, oral histories and par-ticipant observation, produced a wealth of detailed findings. As a study in population movement, it has particularly interesting characteristics as a case of collective migration organized with the purpose of socio-economic improvement and cultural continuity and preservation. The establishment and reproduction of the Welsh ethnic community in Patagonia is argued by Williams to be a 'creation', forged by its members through 'kinship, neighbourliness and mutual aid' (1991: 259, 273–4) in their ongoing strug-gles with the local and national state. Important among these struggles are those required to maintain the economic viability of their settler community.

Williams's study demonstrates the value of a focus on the links between abstract notions of community and the concrete social relations that underpin them. Imagined by its founders as an ethnic community in which the Welsh language and culture could be re-established and renewed in a new geographical context, the Welsh in Chubut province discovered over time that they were not immune to forces of economic and political change that were putting pressures on rural communities the world over. Agricultural producers became subject to adverse economic forces and this meant that many farmers found themselves unable to run their farms profitably, clinging to the land not for financial reasons but because of 'a preference for "security" or "independence,"' that is, a reluctance to take up work as a waged worker, a desire to resist proletarianization. With declining economic power comes greater difficulty in resisting the encroachment of state regulation and control, so the maintenance of Welsh culture came under strain. Over time, 'The language ceased to be the medium of local administration, it was of minimal value for employment, while the agencies of its reproduction were undermined' (1991: 272, 273). Welsh speaking declined among younger generations, and was further marginalized by non-Welsh in-migration into the area. Thus economic, political and demographic forces all played a part in forcing the community to struggle and actively to contest in order to preserve its distinctiveness, in the general context of a sense of loss and decline. This analysis bears closer scrutiny than the misleading stereotypical understandings of the community held by outsiders, and that in itself is a useful corrective. James Hunter's book *The Making of the Crofting Community*, described as 'an attempt to write the modern history of the Gaelic Highlands from the crofting community's point of view' (1976: 5), offers a similar rationale for the detailed study of the centuries-long processes by which contemporary communities have been forged, often in adversity.

4.3 The capacity to surprise

Drawing on the phrase of Claude Lévi-Strauss, David Morgan has written that 'community studies are still "good to think with"' (2005: 655). Like all research, community studies are intended to produce findings that are useful and interesting, and in the process they influence our perception of the world, sometimes in surprising ways (rather than simply confirming our previous understanding). Studies of suburbia provide a good example, revealing that the popular stereotype of dull conformity is wide of the mark. Keller's account of Twin Rivers notes that the development 'promised to recapture something of the traditional sense of community that would have an appeal to residents beyond immediate practical interests'. Expectations of people moving in as pioneers in the 1970s were not necessarily met, especially for those who were disappointed when the reality fell short of their 'dreams of unparalleled family togetherness, opportunities for the children, the promise of new friendships, and an exciting social life'. Over time, however, patterns of sociability developed, between people who shared interests (including shared interests brought about through children, described as 'great social magnets'), religious affiliations or places of origin. Keller argues that these ties generate a sense of shared identity sufficiently strong to withstand the familiar corrosive effects on community endeavours of 'free riders' and 'factional disputes'. That said, she also observes that once a community has emerged 'there is pressure to conform to group norms' (2003: 58, 77, 129, 287, 262), and that the balance between sociability and privacy was not achieved to everyone's satisfaction. Overall, the surprising finding remains that the residents of the suburb sustain greater depth to their social lives than conventional portrayals of suburbia suggest, and by challenging stereotypes researchers can take readers into surprising new understandings.

This is not to say that all the evidence points uniformly in this direction. In some research, suburbs appear to have little conflict because it is easier to acquiesce to the prevailing 'moral order', or to move out (Baumgartner 1988), or because physical presence in suburbs has declined as women's employment has grown (Richards 1990). Prompted by these contradictory findings generated by different studies of individual places, Mary Corcoran and her colleagues developed a multi-method research design incorporating four locations in the Greater Dublin area that captures 'suburban variation'; suburbs are not all the same, and nor are they the exclusive preserve of the middle classes. The study was conceived as being 'of relevance not only to social scientists, but also to architects, planners, policymakers, and the general public', and the timing of the research during an unprecedentedly buoyant housing market makes it a particularly instructive study in comparative perspective. Another unusual feature of the study is its concern to give voice to the children of the suburbs, and there is much to be learned about how eleven-and twelve-year-olds regard the suburban world. Alongside the intriguing finding that the presence of children promotes sociability among adults is the preference expressed by the children for suburban life over urban life. The study's general conclusion is that 'what matters to people is not intimacy with known others in their locality, but loose connections or affiliations' (2010: 257, xvii, xx), within the overall context of an attachment to place that is surprisingly high when set against the prevailing disdain for suburban life that is found in commonplace commentaries. People make positive decisions to move to the suburbs despite the negative stereotypes of social and cultural life there, and sufficient differentiation exists between suburbs to allow scope for people to seek out the particular suburban location most suited to their aspirations.

The finding of people making a positive decision to move to the suburbs has its counterpart in other research showing younger adults moving in the opposite direction for the purpose of escaping suburbia. Tim Butler and Garry Robson's investigation into inner-city gentrification in six areas of London traces the journeys of the grown-up children of middle-class suburbanites to inner-city neighbourhoods that 'provided the excitement and cultural buzz that had been so lacking in many of their childhoods and had been awakened by the experience of being at university'. This is more than a life-stage phenomenon, because these middle-class gentrifiers of inner London stay on when they themselves become parents, preferring to raise their families there than to follow the norm of moving to more sedate suburban surroundings. Butler and Robson show that they do this within communities made up of people with whom they identify, referred to extensively as 'people like us', contexts that allow them to live 'distinctively in ordinary settings' (2003: 163, 108, 18). This desire to locate themselves in neighbourhoods populated by others sharing similar cultural tastes touches on the paradoxical feature of community life whereby it is at once ordinary to the people who are inside it and distinctive from the ways of life of outsiders, including former inner-city residents whose more limited resources make them vulnerable to being displaced by gentrification. Like Mike Savage and his colleagues' (2005) study of four suburban areas in the Greater Manchester area, Butler and Robson note that the processes of globalization and associated geographical mobility have disrupted older patterns of relating to localities, but with the surprising result that people have found new ways of developing a 'narrative of belonging' (2003: 190) to frame accounts of their lives in their chosen surroundings. Purely functional relationships to place do not figure in people's stories of living in contemporary suburbia nor in gentrified inner-city settings.

The point about belonging continuing to be important in the age of globalization applies at least as much to poorer people as it does to the middle-class participants in Butler and Robson's and Savage and his colleagues' studies. Foster's research in London's *Docklands*, coincidentally one of Butler and Robson's research locations, found it 'understandable that not all Isle of Dogs residents were rushing to embrace change' (1999: 306), and suggested that notions of belonging are contested between established residents and newcomers. Geoff Dench and his colleagues developed this theme in their restudy of East London, and in broaching the vexed issue of racial hostility of the white working class to the Bangladeshi in-migrants who had arrived since Young and Willmott's original research they found to their surprise that it was 'the local granny – the archetypal East End "Mum" and heroine of Family and Kinship in East London' who was the most hostile. Perhaps more surprising still to readers is the argument advanced that in-migration by young professionals has exacerbated social divisions, representing a 'class gap' that 'may be even more significant than the cultural divide between the Bangladeshi newcomers and the old white working-class residents in the area, most of whom are the offspring of previous immigrants'. Dench and his colleagues suggest that resentment of gentrification taps into a long-standing inversion of conventional ranking of occupations in which working-class residents of East London 'treated middle-class professions as unimportant or parasitical' (2006: 187, 24, 189), as a way of maintaining self-respect. A history of hostility to the arrival of groups designated 'outsiders' is a recognized feature of many communities including this one (Crow and Allan 1994: ch.4; Mumford and Power 2003: 24), attributable at least in part to competing claims to scarce resources such as housing and employment.

Researchers who set out to investigate communities of which they are not members have to negotiate their status as 'outsiders'. They need to be mindful of potential insensitivity to the 'subtle discriminations' (Cohen 1987: 14) that are found in any culture but that may not be immediately apparent. Cohen's study of the Shetland island of *Whalsay* acknowledges the insights derived from Erving Goffman's (1969: 25) observations on the nearby island of Unst about how people presented themselves to others, drawing out the significance of encounters in which embarrassment occurs. The story recounted by Pahl about how he was 'shown on a number of occasions how a crude drawing of East Anglia and the Thames Estuary could demonstrate that "Sheppey was a piece of shit in the arse 'ole of England"' serves to make the point that Islanders were aware of how outsiders might look down on them, to which they responded by adopting 'a mocking, self-deprecating tone often hiding fierce pride' (1984: 189).

The opening sentence of *The New East End*, 'The East End of London is the backside of the City' (Dench, Gavron and Young 2006: 1), conveys a similar message. Care needs to be taken with apparently derogatory statements that people make about their communities. The original study of the mining community of 'Ashton' reproduced the common assessment by outsiders of the town as 'that dirty hole' (Dennis, Henriques and Slaughter 1969: 12), but in the restudy Dennis Warwick and Gary Littlejohn comment that several participants found fault with the first book because 'outsiders continually get the place and its people all wrong' (1992: 33). As they note, this raises in acute form the question of how community researchers go about their task, and what it is appropriate to conclude when their reports are contested by the very members of the communities being described.

Restudies have the capacity to shed light on how community studies have been received by the participants. Art Gallaher returned to 'Plainville', Missouri, which had previously been studied by James West. West told Gallaher that 'to the best of his knowledge, with one outstanding exception most Plainvillers had taken his report "with relative composure,"' but Gallaher had people saying to him, 'I certainly hope you are not here to do the same thing that feller West did a few years ago. ... Folks here are mighty unhappy with him. ... Some would like to lynch him.' Even the more favourably disposed residents were unsure: 'A nice guy, *but he asked a hell of a lot of questions*' (Gallaher 1971: 286, 288–9, emphasis in original). The feelings of some townspeople that their trust had been betrayed have been echoed in other studies, such as 'Ashton' (Warwick and Littlejohn 1992: 32) and 'Springdale' (Vidich and Bensman 2000: xxxii). Nancy Scheper-Hughes discovered on a return visit to her fieldwork site in Ireland that several locals had not taken kindly to her study, *Saints, Scholars and Schizophrenics*, which offered a sympathetic yet critical analysis of mental illness in the context of rural community decline. Her return was prompted in part by a sense that her approach may have led her to 'an overly critical view of village life in the mid-1970s' (2001: 320), but more than two decades on from the book's original publication a feeling of hurt remained. Critical social science is not always welcome, although it may be, as *The Other Side of Middletown* demonstrates; on yet other occasions people appear 'supremely unaffected' (Bryson and Winter 1999: 69) by the experience of having been studied. The evaluation of community studies' worthwhileness is a complicated matter.

5 Criticisms and defences

The preceding chapters have shown that community studies have their advocates, but also their critics. The views expressed that 'the genre of community studies is currently in crisis' (Savage, Bagnall and Longhurst 2005: 29) and that we may have witnessed 'the death of community studies' (Day 2006: 50) indicate that the criticisms levelled at work in this tradition need to be taken seriously if community studies are to offer a viable approach for future social scientific research. Many of the points at issue are not new. Challenges to the community studies approach go back several decades (Bell 1977; Bell and Newby 1971, 1974; Brook and Finn 1978; Frankenberg 1976; Stacey 1969; Vidich, Bensman and Stein 1971). Nor should it be assumed that researchers located by others in the community studies tradition necessarily saw themselves as part of a common endeavour; there has been criticism from within. In concluding their book on 'Ashton' that has often been treated as an exemplar, Dennis and his colleagues were keen to distance their account from the error that they detected in 'modern functional anthropology' (1969: 246) of neglecting national influences on local life. At other points in the history of the field, attempts to reorient the practice of doing a community study have been made. For example, Wellman and his colleagues argued confidently that their reconceptualization of communities as networks 'moves "community studies" out of its role as an academic sideshow and into the heart of sociology' (1988: 131). Proposals to fundamentally rethink community studies would not have been needed had all been well with the existing body of work; evidently it was not. This chapter will explore the criticisms of community studies, and the responses that have been made to them in recent years, under five broad themes. These are that community studies are variously too parochial, too static, too positive, too descriptive and too prosaic.

5.1 Are community studies too parochial?

The essence of the first criticism is that community studies focus too much on the specifics of the community under investigation and too little on wider relevance, so that their concerns are 'merely of local interest' (Mills 1959: 368). The network map of kinship connections in Rees's study of rural Wales showed only the linkages within the parish boundary, conveying the impression of an inward-looking community unconnected to the outside world. Rees could not entirely avoid acknowledging the growing influence of wider forces, such as the pull of employment elsewhere, but although the discussion of outmigration offered something of a corrective, the principal focus on the local perspective was reasserted by the comment that 'the bonds of kinship and locality retain their hold upon those who have gone away, and several have returned home to retire' (1951: 76, 148). The disruptive impact on local communities of outside forces presented a serious challenge to researchers whose primary interest was in recording the details of a place and the distinctive way of life of the people who lived there. Stacey, who also used network mapping to trace connections within her fieldwork site, found her remit 'to study the social structure and culture of Banbury' so dominated by immigration (as people from elsewhere made those born in the town a minority) that traditional 'Banbury society' (1960: v, 17) was becoming progressively less distinctive, and thus less researchable. By the time of the restudy, external influences on the town's social order had further fragmented it to such an extent that 'no single hierarchy of social class or social status' (Stacey et al. 1975: 132) could be found, and Stacey (1969) concluded that the concept of 'community' was of doubtful usefulness.

The titles of many classic community studies do reinforce the impression that the principal purpose of the research was to capture particular expressions of local social life: *The Sociology of an English Village: Gosforth* (Williams 1956), *The People of Ship Street* (Kerr 1956) and *The Tory Islanders* (Fox 1978) serve as examples. These and other studies of communities that stood outside of the modern mainstream could be justified as attempts to follow Lévi-Strauss and record 'cultures sadly but rapidly on the wane' (Scheper-Hughes 2001: xxvii) before the opportunity had disappeared. Such studies offer insights into a bygone age, and although the ways of life described may appear parochial by today's standards, there is still value in the research record that they provide. Parochial in this sense does not necessarily mean unworthwhile, because it furnishes a point of contrast (Stacey et al. 1975: 3). It is interesting and useful to know about remote Gosforth as it was before the establishment of the atomic energy station in the neighbouring parish at Sellafield (Williams 1956: 229); to be aware what traditional working-class family routines were like in slum areas of central Liverpool before urban redevelopment (Kerr 1958); and to be reminded that past patterns of community life in rural Ireland could vary from those described in Arensberg and Kimball's classic account (Fox 1978: xi). Local studies do not have to be of only local interest.

A second response to the charge of community studies' parochialism is to note the growth in studies that have explored international and even global connectedness. Such a perspective was already present early on in the key Chicago School study of migration to the United States from Poland (Thomas and Znaniecki 1927). In addition to examples discussed above that extended this theme such as the British in Spain (O'Reilly 2000a), Welsh settlement in Argentina (Williams 1991) and the Bangladeshis in London (Foster 1999; Dench, Gavron and Young 2006) and Swansea (Charles, Davies and Harris 2008), the idea of transnational communities is advanced by Peggy Levitt (2001) through research into migration flows between the Dominican Republic and Boston, Massachusetts. Her book, *The Transnational Villagers*, implicitly develops Gans's (1962b) theme of urban villagers, which had also been based on Boston fieldwork. The patterns of movement back and forth between the two places that Levitt traces involve people 'keeping feet in both worlds'. This is not only the familiar story of migrant workers sending back remittances to kinsfolk in their country of origin; people's active engagement in 'social relationships that span two settings' and their sense of membership of a transnational community that obliges them to 'do right' by that community are also described. Levitt's reference to 'global culture at the local level' (2001: 21, 10–11) reminds us that local does not have to be parochial. A rather different study makes the same point through an image of global connectedness linking a mile-long street in London (Walworth Road) with the more than twenty countries of origin in Asia, Africa, Europe and the Americas of the shopkeepers who have settled there (Hall 2012: 34). The contrast with Rees's parish-bound network could not be starker.

The criticism of community studies as parochial raises the key methodological issue of the unit of analysis that is employed. There are many instances of 'community' being treated as synonymous with a particular place, sometimes as large as a town or as small as a street, with parishes, villages, neighbourhoods or islands providing other geographically bounded foci of attention. Pahl grappled with this issue on Sheppey, where the survey that he commissioned provided an overview of the whole island but 'could not pick up the contours of small, relatively self-contained social worlds'. He was mindful 'that these distinctive residential areas very often have different cultural styles and traditions', which would have been revealed by 'an intensive survey of a few streets' had his team undertaken one. In one place he refers to the island as 'a small community', in another to the island's 'communities' plural (1984: 182, 173, 155). Douglas Harper has been critical of community research projects that take for granted that community relationships are contained within administrative boundaries, noting that this is a problematic assumption for the types of research he has undertaken. Studying the tramp community whose members are constantly on the move led him to conclude that 'community, in this case, more accurately described bundles of cultural expectations than populations in a location'. He learned the criteria by which membership of the tramp community could be identified, and that sociologists who equated homeless people with the permanent population of 'skid row' were operating with extremely partial understanding of the community. His next study was likewise provocative, focusing on one rural mechanic, 'Willie', in upstate New York and the network of reciprocal relationships built up around him. Harper treats it as a normative community, notwithstanding the fact that it would not be 'discernible through censuses' (1992: 143, 144, 146). Both projects are instances of community case studies, and both force the recognition that community relationships go beyond bureaucratic categories, and invite us to rethink what we understand by a 'case'.

Harper's study of Willie's network uses a way of getting at community that is parochial only up to the point that the reader realizes that this is a case study of resilience in the face of change being wrought in a traditional world (1987: 166). One individual's story can speak for a much broader body of people, just as Pahl used Linda and Jim to do. In a different fashion, but following the same principle, is Wellman's use of his own engagement with the virtual world to illustrate what can be learned from the method of tracing ego-centric networks, such as his involvement in Twitter (Gruzd, Wellman and Takhteyev 2011). This is one way to 'build a theory of community' (Harper 1992: 139), moving from the individual case towards larger categories. Another approach is to build comparison into research design so that points of similarity and difference can be drawn out from different communities in which the same methods of investigation have been employed. Whereas the original 'Ashton' study presented an undifferentiated picture, the restudy by Warwick and Littlejohn (1992) reported on its findings broken down into four localities that presented variations on the culture of mining communities. St Leger and Gillespie's (1991) comparison of care in three areas of Belfast, Butler and Robson's (2003) exploration of the meaning of gentrification in six parts of inner London, Savage, Bagnall and Longhurst (2005) study of place, neighbourhood and community in four areas of Greater Manchester, Corcoran and her colleagues' use of four Dublin suburbs to convey suburban diversity and Marilyn Porter's (1993) contrasting accounts of women's work in three Newfoundland communities are further examples of this approach. Rosser and Harris's (1965) analyses of the contrasts between the four neighbourhoods in Swansea had already demonstrated the value of this technique. It was used again to good effect in the restudy (Charles, Davies and Harris 2008) to show the city's diversity, in the process providing an effective counter to the criticism that community studies produce only parochial knowledge.

5.2 Are community studies too static?

Alongside the criticism that community studies focus on people in only one particular place that is of limited interest is the related criticism that they focus on only one moment in time, and in doing so fail to capture the essential dynamism of community relationships. This criticism was advanced by scholars who associated community studies with a functionalist approach to social research. This treated phenomena under investigation as integrated wholes whose various parts were in a state of balance within a social system that had a tendency towards equilibrium. Thomas Eriksen has highlighted the powerful tradition in social and cultural anthropology of emphasizing 'the study of interrelationships and sociocultural wholes' (2001: 257), and this undoubtedly left its mark on many classic community studies. The *Yankee City* study treated community as a '"working whole" in which each part had definite functions which had to be performed, or substitutes acquired, if the whole society was to maintain itself' (Warner and Lund 1941: 14). The reorientation required to appreciate that 'societies or cultures are not tightly integrated, unchanging or closed systems' (Eriksen 2001: 257) took a long time. It involved numerous innovations in both theory and method, within anthropology and beyond. These developments have demonstrated the capacity of community studies to accommodate both movement and change.

The mobility of Harper's (1982) tramp community and Levitt's (2001) transnational community discussed in the previous section have echoes in a number of other studies. These include Alice Goffman's 'fugitive community' (2014: 195) of young black men in urban America, Judith Okely's (1983) traveller-gypsies whose preference is not to lead a settled life in one place, and the less obvious but still real mobilities of Ben Rogaly and Becky Taylor's housing estate residents whose lives were characterized less by immobility than by 'flux' (2011: 180). Another example would be the networks of musical connection that took Ruth Finnegan's new town residents away from their immediate neighbours during their leisure time and along 'pathways in urban living' (1989: ch.21) towards others with shared cultural tastes. Appreciation of the significance of mobility can be found in earlier studies, such as Rosser and Harris's account of 'families in a mobile society', which explored the connections between social and geographical mobility as social trends unfolded, taking people away from 'the Cohesive Society: small in scale, limited and narrow in its social horizons, homogeneous in social composition, familiar and familistic, with a strong community consciousness generated by common residence and common necessity' (1965: 15). This study concluded that family and kinship networks within communities could adjust to emerging patterns of geographical mobility, engaging with the ideas of the functionalist theorist Talcott Parsons in the process. The restudy also directed attention to 'continuity in the face of change' and cast doubt on the idea that 'the "local community" has disappeared' (2008: 58, 228). The earlier study had pointed out that the traditional working-class communities that had grown up around iron and steel works and coal mines had been made up of migrants from the surrounding countryside and beyond; geographical mobility had been present before the mobile society.

Conducting a restudy is one way in which researchers can rebut the criticism that community studies are too static. Community restudies go back to the Lynds' return to Muncie to produce *Middletown in Transition* (Lynd and Lynd 1937), and other titles also convey their capacity to capture shifts that have occurred in the interim: *Power, Persistence and Change*

(Stacey et al. 1975), *Affluent Workers Revisited* (Devine 1992), *Social Change, Suburban Lives* (Bryson and Winter 1999), *The New East End* (Dench, Gavron and Young 2006) and *Families in Transition* (Charles, Davies and Harris 2008). Returning to a community has the potential to reveal the dynamic nature of community relationships. Such work has to confront the challenge of differentiating social change in community relationships from changes to the analytical frameworks used to capture them – what Colin Bell in his discussion of the Banbury restudy referred to as the distinction between 'social change' and 'sociological change' (1977: 60). This is an issue even where the return to the field happens within only a few years of the original study, but is obviously all the greater when longer periods have elapsed. Nor should researchers fall into the trap of looking only for change in community relationships, because dynamic processes can result in the reproduction of social arrangements, as the reference to 'persistence' in the Banbury study implies. The comment by Charles and her colleagues that continuity in family practices constitutes their Swansea restudy's 'most striking finding' (2008: 224) makes this point well.

A sense of history, including continuities as well as changes, can also be conveyed by community studies that include historical context. Pahl devotes a whole chapter to doing this for Sheppey (1984: ch.6), as do Goodall and Campbell for the history over two centuries of Muncie's black community (Lassiter et al. 2004: ch.2). Vidich and Bensman cover a similar time frame in describing the 'social, economic and historical setting' of Springdale (2000: ch.1), as does Jeremy Tunstall's (1969: ch.1) account of the development of the Hull fishing community; other examples of such contextualization are Blokland's account of 'the origins of Hillesluis' in Rotterdam as 'a heterogeneous working-class district' (2003: 21), Max Farrar's 'brief history of migration to Chapeltown' (2002: ch.3) that sets the scene for multi-ethnic relations in Leeds between people who had moved there from the Caribbean, South Asia, Eastern Europe and across the four nations of the UK, and Levitt's (2001: ch.1) historical narrative of migration across the Americas. History is even more central to Williams's (1991) analysis of the Welsh in Patagonia, and in Harper's narration of change in rural communities in the half century since the archived photographs that provide the historical record on which he focuses were taken. The visual record of farm life in the 1940s provides an insight into a lost age when neighbours' co-operation in undertaking work was not only rational from an economic point of view but also had a ritual quality to it, and 'integrated the group, reaffirmed collective values, and created the basis for shared understanding of experience'. Harper acknowledges Durkheim's ideas in this discussion of how the rituals of shared work reinforced bonds of community 'outside the larger culture of individualistic, competitive capitalism' (2001: 181). He also recognizes the need to explain how such a dramatic change could occur in such a short period, historically speaking, and does so by reference to how technological innovation had unfolded in the American context.

Not only are community studies able to accommodate change, it can also be argued that they illuminate large-scale processes of change unfolding in particular community contexts (Crow 2002b). These include the impact of various social scientific themes such as industrialization (Williams 1991), deindustrialization (Harris 1987; Pahl 1984; Pappas 1989; Wight 1993), proletarianization (Williams 1981), militarization (Giarchi 1984), secularization (Littlejohn 1963), medicalization (Cornwell 1984), inferiorization (Dempsey 1992), privatization (Blokland 2003; Devine 1992), counterurbanization (Benson 2011), suburbanization (Berger 1968; Bryson and Winter 1999; Gans 1967; Keller 2003; Richards 1990; Seeley, Sim and Loosley 1963), Jamaicanization (McKenzie 2015) and globalization (Eade 1997; Foster 1999; Levitt 2001; Savage, Bagnall and Longhurst 2005). In the development of such analyses, researchers are able to draw on the findings of previous generations of community studies but also on the growing body of work about community relationships in times past that oral historians have produced. These studies are important not only for their intrinsic interest but also as a source of research questions that comparative perspectives throw up. Trevor Lummis's account of East Anglian fishing communities around 1900 contains the telling observation that these were working-class communities possessed of solidarity largely through the 'mutual aid ... constructed and operated by women' (1985: 167). The broader companion study in which Lummis was also involved makes the related point about women's 'crucial role in social change' (Thompson, Wailey and Lummis 1983: 181), that it is mothers who are the primary influence on the attitudes and understandings of new generations. Lynn Jamieson and Claire Toynbee's study of growing up in early-twentieth-century rural Scotland ends by reflecting on how things are different now, and why, with the arrival of 'the incomer population of migrants from the towns' (1992: 217) constituting a strong element in any explanation of change.

5.3 Are community studies too positive?

One of the key arguments in favour of community studies advanced by Lodewijk Brunt is that they allow researchers to get beyond the 'public face' that is 'presented to the outside world' (2001: 84), and to access what lies behind. This is a contested claim. Critics of community studies argue the opposite, that there is a tendency for researchers to be persuaded by partial and romanticized accounts of how community relationships operate, that is, to be taken in by the myths presented to them. The criticism of the ICS for directing attention to the warmth of the traditional working-class community of East London, and in particular for eulogizing the matriarchal 'Mum' character as the pivotal figure in such communities (Cornwell 1984: 24), has parallels with criticisms of oral historians being misled by the selectivity of their respondents' memories. Not for nothing did Payne cast doubt on community researchers' capacity to capture the less attractive sides of community about which people are more reluctant to speak: violence and conflict, prejudice and intolerance, inequality and exclusion. As a consequence, Payne writes, the result 'is a sociological portrait of communities that is a flattering one' (1996: 23). Such overly positive accounts may be attributable to poor practice by researchers who gravitate towards respondents with whom they feel more comfortable, but it may also reflect a bias inherent in the very concept of 'community', which Raymond Williams has described as a 'warmly persuasive word' that 'seems never to be used unfavourably' (1983: 76). These are both plausible reasons why community studies may present their subject matter too positively.

At one level the charge of community studies being too positive is easily contested. The titles of several monographs include the word 'conflict' (Dench, Gavron and Young 2006, Foster 1999, Rex and Moore 1967), and others carry indications of social problems such as 'dispute' (Waddington, Wykes and Critcher 1991), *Turf Wars* (Modan 2007), 'redundancy' (Harris 1987), 'poverty' (Coates and Silburn 1973), 'social exclusion' (Smith 2005), 'decline' (Brody 1973), 'ruination' (Mah 2012) and *Endless Pressure* (Pryce 1979). Arguably the bravest choice in relation to titles was Scheper-Hughes's inclusion of 'schizophrenia' in her book on rural Ireland, given the stigma attached to mental illness. Prompted by a desire 'to bring out of the shadows a hidden dimension of social life' that constituted 'a collective social tragedy', the study examines 'the costs of loyalty to family and village' that fell on those left behind in the oppressive world in which the demands of 'family, Church and community' placed an intolerable burden on many individuals. The opinion that the Durkheimian concept of 'anomie' described 'the emotional state of a majority of Ballybran villagers' (2001: 46, 33, 50, 122) was not judgemental, but a statement of just how problematic local social relations were. This was quite the opposite of an unduly positive representation. It stood in sharp contrast to 'the harmony of the rural social system' (Brody 1973: 6) that Arensberg and Kimball's classic study of the Irish countryside had celebrated, inappropriately in the eyes of several later researchers.

What is true of some titles is even more true of the substance of many studies. Pahl's (1984) Sheppey study is an account of social polarization, and in *The Other Side of Middletown* Lassiter and his colleagues (2004) tell a story of racial separateness, if not segregation. Both of these sets of findings appear to contradict the essence of community as a phenomenon of positive togetherness, but they make greater sense when the capacity of communities to accommodate division is explored further. Ken Dempsey's study of *Smalltown* in rural Australia notes that residents hold a favourable image of themselves as 'one big happy family', but it goes on to show that this rhetoric is at odds with the presence of 'marginality and antagonism'. This extends beyond familiar categories of deviants such as 'no-hopers' (people with problematic relationships to alcohol, gambling and personal hygiene), and 'blockies' (people in substandard housing and in a precarious economic situation), to include the 'marginalization of non-deviants' such as newcomers who experience difficulty breaking into established social networks, and the elderly. The reality of life in *Smalltown* is thus at odds with the professed belief in 'egalitarianism and the Gemeinschaft-like characteristics of caring, fairness and honesty' (1990: chs 3-4, 53). *Smalltown* residents perceive life there to be 'superior physically, socially and emotionally to life in many other places, and especially to life in the city' (Dempsey 1992: 25). This is not an isolated finding. It echoes, for example, the discrepancies that Vidich and Bensman found between the images of themselves as 'just plain folks' who are 'all equal' that the residents of Springdale held and the realities of division expressed through the 'universal derision' with which 'the shack people' (2000: ch.2, 69) are regarded. Vidich and Bensman's message was received no better by the townspeople of Springdale than Scheper-Hughes's had been by her villagers; in both cases community members were unhappy with their negative representation.

Failure of communities in practice to meet aspirations of togetherness and mutual supportiveness ought not to be that surprising a finding given the potential of community relationships, either present or past, to be idealized. Unrealistically positive ideas about community have been fostered by the use of idealizations of the past as 'a stick to beat the present' (Williams 1975: 21), that is, a point of comparison to highlight today's purportedly lamentable state by emphasizing the theme of the 'loss of community' (Lee and Newby 1983: ch.4). Scrutiny of the historical record has raised awkward questions for the loss of community thesis by unearthing evidence of the less attractive features of violence, intolerance, hostility towards outsiders and resistance to change. Traditional working-class community life was not all reciprocity and solidarity (Crow and Allan 1994: ch.2). Blokland reports that in 'the allegedly cohesive working-class neighbourhood' of early-twentieth-century Hillesluis, 'neighbour relations used to be inevitable and exacted a heavy toll if they were bad'. Paradoxically, she suggests, the loss of community thesis can be inverted for some present-day individuals: 'Now that people are less dependent on fellow neighbourhood residents for social support, and networks are less locally embedded, some people have managed to develop intimate bonds with fellow neighbourhood residents that used to be harder to establish' (2003: 27, 14–15, 214). The message here is that the symbolism of community is open to reworking in each generation, and it follows that idealization of community relationships is not restricted to the past.

O'Reilly's (2000a) study of British migrants to Spain provides a good example of how belief in the loss of community in their country of origin is compatible with a conviction that positive community relationships await them in their new home. Compared to the participants in O'Reilly's study Michaela Benson's British migrants to rural France were more middle-class, but they were similarly motivated by 'their imaginings of a better way of life', in this case revolving more around integration into the local host community. They are described as pursuing 'an imagined community' that was expected to 'provide them with the antidote to their malaise with life in contemporary Britain' (2011: 80, 45). The story of discrepancies between expectations and lived realities has much in common with other research findings about the pursuit of community as an ongoing quest of migrants to belong to their new environment. The literature on relations between community insiders and outsiders is by no means all positive, in the sense that outsiders can find themselves excluded and stigmatized, or at least accepted as full members of their new communities only after a probationary period, sometimes quite prolonged (Crow and Maclean 2013). This phenomenon is most extensively documented for place-based communities, but it has also been noted for internet communities (Hornsby 2013), among others. When prolonged exclusion is encountered by outsiders they may retreat into an encapsulated community, set apart from the mainstream (Anwar 1985: ch.11), and this fate may also befall local populations where in-migration is numerically dominant (Newby et al. 1978: 194). Community studies that report on such segregation cannot be regarded as unduly positive.

5.4 Are community studies too descriptive?

The difficulties with theory that community researchers have encountered are well known. Work in the Chicago School tradition was criticized on the grounds that it often 'consisted of lengthy, detailed descriptions which resulted in very small amounts of theory, if any' (Glaser and Strauss 1967: 15). Conversely, Tönnies's distinction between *gemeinschaft* and *gesellschaft* was framed at the very general level that characterized much nineteenth-century theorization, and its simplification into the rural–urban continuum had become unsustainable by the 1960s. Functionalist theories of communities as 'natural' wholes fared little better, since the underpinning concept of equilibrium meant that they had difficulty in dealing with either conflict or change. Elias's comment that 'the theoretical aspects of community studies are less advanced than the empirical work in that field' (1974: ix) underplayed the problem, perhaps because he was mindful that his own approach offered one solution. In their analysis of Winston Parva, Elias and Scotson's challenge had been to account for the surprising fact that 'the inhabitants of one part thought of themselves as vastly superior to those of the other'. Elias saw in Scotson's MA thesis research 'a vehicle for the development of his own theorising' (Mennell 1992: 116). The theory of what Elias called the 'established-outsider figuration' had applicability far beyond this one suburb, and related to the processes by which social superiority and inferiority are reproduced, including the acceptance of this state of affairs by those marked out as inferior. The exercise of power to exclude and to stigmatize, and to excuse the presence of shortcomings among members of the dominant group, appeared sufficiently familiar from other studies that Elias could even countenance the model containing elements that were 'universal' (Elias 1994: xvii, xvi, xvii). Elias's recommended focus on 'the specific interdependencies between people who form with each other that kind of figuration that we call a community' (1974: xvii) has some similarity to the analysis of the structuring of social relationships through networks, and the conclusion that the people involved resembled 'puppets on a string' (1994: lii) confirms the importance attached by this approach to structure.

Elias's approach has not in practice been a particularly prominent influence on more recent community research, at least not directly. It can, however, be regarded as having some effect through the ideas of Pierre Bourdieu and the development of thinking about gender. Elias's attention to the interdependencies between members of communities did highlight the necessary connectedness between both 'I' and 'we' (1991: Pt III) and 'we' and 'they' (1978: 130), but Bourdieu's attention to distinction has more resonance with the focus on the appeal of community's exclusivity. It has been noted already that the quest to live among 'people like us' comes through strongly in studies of middle-class mobility (Benson 2011; Butler and Robson 2003; Savage, Bagnall and Longhurst 2005), but the desire to share residential space with people perceived to be similar in terms of cultural capital is a more general one. In the final publication from the Sheppey project, Pahl and Wallace quote the working-class participant who was unhappy with the fact that 'a lot of the people round here, they are not our type of people' (1988: 139) and interpret it as contemporary evidence of the familiar distinction between rough and respectable lifestyles. Other studies that draw on Bourdieu include Warwick and Littlejohn's deployment of the idea of 'local cultural capital' (1992: 15), Wight's analysis of 'taste' (1993: 121), Lennart Roselund's account of 'distinction' expressed as 'spatial differentiation' (2009: 304), Charles and her colleagues' focus on the role of social reproduction in understanding 'processes of change and continuity' (2008: 230); Scheper-Hughes's (2001: 43–6) comparison of her fieldwork site with Bourdieu's Béarn; Simon Charlesworth's (2000) exploration of working-class stigmatization; and Lisa McKenzie's use of the concept of 'habitus' to help in understanding 'how negative namings and stigmatised positions can be absorbed into an identity' (2015: 206). It is not difficult to find echoes of Elias's thinking in any of these analyses, but the implication is that Bourdieu's concepts take them further. The influence of Elias can also be traced on the reorientation of community studies in relation to gender. The observation in *The Established and the Outsiders* that 'it is difficult to imagine communities without women and children, though one can imagine communities almost without men' (Elias and Scotson 1994: 146–7) gave impetus, along with other prompts such as that from Frankenberg (1976), to researchers concerned to explain community's gendered character. At one level what was required was an updating of accounts in the context of the growth of women's employment, as noted for example by Bryson and Winter's (1999) restudy. Bennett Berger's working-class suburb had been 'manless during the day' (1968: 6), but Lyn Richards found dual-income households meant that *Nobody's Home*. She also found that the move away from the male breadwinner type of household that had been predominant in the era of the classic community studies did not herald the changed domestic power relations that might have been expected to follow. Gendered differences in labour market opportunities and rewards stood as one obstacle to greater equality between partners, but so did the fact that 'home' continued to mean 'very different things to men and women', and the same point applied to 'community'. In relation to the latter, Richards criticized previous researchers for overlooking 'women's local relationships as work', and highlighted in particular the importance of women's contributions to everyday neighbouring and 'network management' (1990: 135, 180, 182). In Newfoundland, Porter was discovering 'how invisible much women's work was, especially caring or health-related work' (1993: 130). These studies took Pahl's (1984) extension of the definition of 'work' one step further, and the focus on neighbouring chimed with developments elsewhere.

Abrams's investigations into neighbouring are particularly pertinent to the discussion of the role of theory in community research. His findings included women's greater involvement in neighbouring and also that men had a different style of relating to their neighbours that involved 'help with specific problems' that contrasted with the deeper relationships cultivated by women. Elias might have understood this as evidence that what he called 'the We-I balance' (1991: Pt III) is gendered. Following Durkheim, Abrams regarded solidarity as 'the most interesting element of social relationships' but also like Durkheim found it a difficult concept to operationalize, unsure whether to focus on solidarity as 'intensity, style of transaction, density, "multiplexity", range, frequency of contact, location of contact and clustering' (Bulmer 1986: 76, 33–4). A person could have extensive contact with a neighbour without the content of the interaction necessarily having great significance, for example, and the motivation to engage with neighbours could be more or less altruistic. Abrams had already grappled with these challenges in his study of communes with McCulloch, which sought to explore the conditions under which 'people want to do what they have got to do'. This study pointed in addition to the methodological conclusion that attempting to get at these issues through a questionnaire was 'naïve', and that better-quality data came through the development of friendships which generated 'more detailed, intimate and probably reliable information' (1976: 154, 222, 226), albeit that the use of these data in turn raised the problem of consent. This problem contributed to Abrams's conclusion about research into neighbour networks that they may be hard 'to get to know from within' (Bulmer 1986: 251), but the thrust of his argument was nevertheless that analysis of networks offered a promising way forward in the study of informal social relations (Bulmer 1985).

There are plenty of examples of recent community studies using the concept of social networks, often in conjunction with the concept of social capital (Blokland and Savage 2008; Charles, Davies and Harris 2008; Corcoran, Gray and Peillon 2010, Levitt 2001, Phillipson et al. 2001, Savage, Bagnall and Longhurst 2005), or related concepts such as social support (Richards 1990). These help to meet the first part of the criticism of the community studies tradition as 'atheoretical and uncumulative' (Pahl 1980: 1), but the second element is less easily countered. Leaving aside that not all studies that employed the concept of social networks had generated their data through social network analysis, which has developed rigorous and sophisticated methodological procedures (Scott 2012), the problem that the concept of social capital has roots in the work of Bourdieu, Putnam and Coleman and that these theoretical frameworks are not readily compatible has to be confronted (Fine 2010: ch.3). Put another way, while it may be accepted that community studies have previously been guilty of following an atheoretical approach, there can also be dangers in adopting theoretical ideas that point in different directions because of their diverse origins in traditions of thought that can be traced back respectively to Marx, de Tocqueville and rational choice theory.

For some researchers the attraction of social capital and social network approaches is their openness to quantification, and thus the measurement of the patterns of reciprocal exchange. However, analyses of such phenomena are only as good as the data on which they are based, and more sophisticated concepts alone would not have helped Pahl when both survey and interview data from the Sheppey project 'suggested that people typically claimed that they did more informal work for others than they received themselves' (1984: 250). This finding is unconvincing because, in the round, giving and taking must balance, but it is a common finding nevertheless (Crow, Allan and Summers 2002: 139). Pahl's explanation in terms of people's desire not to appear dependent means that the familiar methodological challenge remains of what people say that they do not necessarily corresponding to what they actually do. It does not follow that researchers are unable to draw any conclusions, and Corcoran and her colleagues (2010) report variations in patterns of social capital in their four fieldwork sites, while Charles and her colleagues are confident enough to declare that, for Swansea, 'claims about the decline of social capital ... are, at the very least, premature' (2008: 227). Furthermore, Savage and his colleagues found the concepts of social capital and networks useful in reworking old ideas about community into the notion of 'elective belonging' (2005: 29), which they argue is better suited to understand attachment in the age of globalization.

5.5 Are community studies too prosaic?

The working definition of community studies with which this book began focuses on ordinary people's everyday lives, and it is worth noting that the participants of Savage and his colleagues' (2005: 11) research, and many other studies, emphasize their ordinariness. The stuff of 'community' is necessarily routine and mundane, and community researchers will seek to convey this, but this is not to everyone's taste. Mills, possessing a distinctive style of presenting his ideas (Crow 2005: ch.6), was dismissive in his assessment: 'The endless "community studies" of the sociologists often read like badly written novels' (Mills 1959: 358). It is relevant to note that Pahl considered presenting his Sheppey research as a novel or a film rather than a conventional academic book as the best way of conveying 'the reality of ordinary people's lives' (1984: 8). To this end he included ten photographs of the island and its people, and in doing so followed an established tradition of community studies (Fox 1978; Gans 1962b; Rees

1951; Rex and Moore 1967; Thompson, Wailey and Lummis 1983; Tunstall 1969; Williamson 1982). This tradition of including visual images has continued, and arguably grown in popularity. The centrality of photographs to the work of Lassiter and his colleagues (2004) and of Harper (1987, 2001) has been noted already, but they are also used effectively to give a fuller sense of people and place by many others (Baumann 1996; Benson 2011; Bryson and Winter 1999; Cohen 1987; Corcoran, Gray and Peillon 2010; Dench, Gavron and Young 2006; Finnegan 1989; Foster 1999; Jamieson and Toynbee 1992; Keller 2003; Low 2003; McKenzie 2015; Mah 2012; Modan 2007; Mumford and Power 2003; Nettle 2015; Pappas 1989; Phillipson et al. 2001; Rogaly and Taylor 2011; Rosenlund 2009; Scheper-Hughes 2001; Warwick and Littlejohn 1992). Photographs help to bring the text of community studies to life, and so fit in with the ambition of community researchers to make their work engaging and accessible.

The issue at stake here is the criticism of academic work that courts popularity at the expense of rigour. It was noted in Chapter 2 that the negative evaluation of the output of the ICS for being impressionistic contributed to the decline of community studies in the old tradition, and this tension over the purpose of inquiry has not disappeared. The argument developed in Chapter 4 around efforts to combine research that is both useful and interesting has relevance to the most famous ICS publication, *Family and Kinship in East London*, which had sold over half a million copies by 1992 (Crow and Allan 1994: 24) and was brought out in a new edition fifty years on from the date of the original. In their introduction to the new edition, Kate Gavron (one of the authors of the restudy, *The New East End*, that had come out the previous year) and Geoff Mulgan celebrated Young and Willmott's 'plain language' which contrasted with 'the cultivated obscurity of so much of the sociology of the succeeding decades' (2007: vii). Moreover, it does not follow that the achievement of accessibility has to be at the expense of rigour; and Gavron and Mulgan note how the research for the book was innovative by the standards of the time, including input from Phyllis Willmott (Peter's wife). They also point out that the book was written for an audience of policymakers as well as general lay readers and academics. Arguably it had greater influence on 'strategies of social action rather than ... social research' (Dench, Gavron and Young 2006: 14). One of the lessons for the design of social research was the value of ensuring that the capacity exists to follow up unexpected findings. In their introduction to the 1986 edition of the book, Young and Willmott recall how the original plan had been to investigate housing policy, but 'as happens so often with research, more interesting than what we were seeking was what we stumbled on' (2007: xiv), namely the kinship network that came to be the project's central focus.

Relating how the research process led to unexpected findings can provide the basis of a compelling narrative. There is an element of Young and Willmott taking readers into their confidence by admitting that their research focus had been hit upon 'more or less accidentally' (1957: xvi). Scheper-Hughes has recalled how she 'did not go to Ireland with any intention of seeking out madness', and that 'certain serendipitous events altered the original focus' (2001: 22–3) of her study, including unplanned encounters. Hochschild reports that her participants were 'part of a community I did not expect to find' (1973: xiv). St Leger and Gillespie describe their study aims being as much 'to encounter serendipitous findings as to provide a test of specific hypotheses' (1991: 163), while Pahl admits that at the early stages of his fieldwork he was following 'a rather confused idea' (1984: 9) of the informal economic activity that he would go on to write about in *Divisions of Labour* only after a prolonged period of reassessment. Harper has commented that, 'Sociologists are probably always strangers, in some sense, to the communities that they live in' (1987: 8), and their reports on those communities allow the reader to share the experience of discovering things about people and practices other than their own. Gans had gone to the West End of Boston because he 'wanted to know what a slum was like, and how it felt to live in one' and, mindful of his outsider status, 'tried to describe the way of life of lower level people as they might describe it themselves if they were sociologists' (1962b: ix, x). Such work can be a revelation. Maurice Stein argues that it has the capacity to leave readers 'enthralled', explained by 'the sheer descriptive appeal of the community study' (1964: 96, 97) and the opportunity to become familiar with other people's experience that it provides.

Mills's unfavourable comparison of community studies to novels was reworked in a more qualified fashion by Ruth Glass. Her much-cited reference to 'the poor sociologist's substitute for a novel' applied, she said, to the genre 'too often', but was not universal, since her judgement was that 'distinguished' community studies had also been written, such as the Lynds' *Middletown* books. The problem was that the analytical social scientific element was 'usually missing', leaving reports on research too rooted in the particular case and too little engaged with general processes; to undertake a community study well 'requires a rare combination of empirical and literary skills of a high order' (1989: 86). Written in the 1960s, Glass's critique raised common concerns of the time about comparability and generalizability, but did not rule out the possibility of these concerns being addressed. Indeed, some researchers at the time were doing just this. Rosser and Harris acknowledge 'most valuable help' from the ICS with the planning of their research in Swansea, recognizing comparison to be 'a central necessity for all sociological investigation'. Their report may have begun with an extended account of one case study, that of the Hughes family of Morriston that originated from a meeting 'by chance' early on in the fieldwork, but they go on to set out the need to consider the book's key themes 'in a more general manner' and they do so using a range of different types of data including survey data. They also include the interviewing schedule as an appendix, and a further appendix on 'the representativeness of the sample' (1965: 33, 4, 18, 309–22, 323–6). Other examples of community studies that have used appendices to provide detailed information about the study's methodology include Abrams and McCulloch (1976); Bulmer (1986); Charles, Davies and Harris (2008); Corcoran, Gray and Peillon (2010); Dench, Gavron and Young (2006); Gans (1962b, 1967); Goldthorpe et al. (1969); Holme (1985); Jamieson and Toynbee (1992); Keller (2003); Kerr (1958); Levitt (2001); Lynd and Lynd (1929); Mumford and Power (2003); Newby et al. (1978); Rex and Moore (1967); St Leger and Gillespie (1991); Scheper-Hughes (2001); Seeley et al. (1956); Stacey (1960); Stacey et al. (1975); Tunstall (1969); Wallace (1987) and Whyte (1955). It is only relatively recently that archiving of such material has become standard, and in this sense community studies may be considered among the pioneers of the practice of providing technical details of how social scientific research has been undertaken for other researchers to learn from and in some cases replicate.

The co-operation between different researchers allowed Rosser and Harris to build on Young and Willmott's (1957: 16) finding that twenty-one of forty-five couples began married life living with either the groom's or more frequently the bride's parents, and to report that for a larger sample of 620 Swansea couples, 61.7 per cent had done so in the two decades to 1960. They also showed that starting married life with one or other set of parents was the case for the majority of middle-class as well as working-class couples, and that the percentage of newly-wed couples living on their own declined to 31 per cent from the figure of 52 per cent that applied to the preceding period 1914–39 (Rosser and Harris 1965: 250). Four decades on (reporting 2002 data), Charles and her colleagues found Swansea's extended family households to have 'declined to such an extent as to be insignificant' (2008: 188), constituting a remarkable transformation even without the additional consideration of the shift that occurred over the period from tenancy to owner-occupation as the principal tenure type. It is an even more remarkable change from the situation described by Madeline Kerr where married daughters living with their Mum was an 'ideal custom' (1958: 14). Anthea Holme's (1985: 9) retracing of Young and Willmott's footsteps in East London pointed (via a different indicator) to the same broad direction of travel, with 17 per cent of her one hundred young families sharing accommodation with relatives or friends. Another example of an issue open to comparative investigation through the use of quantitative data is that of length of time a person lives in the same property. Charles and her colleagues (2008: 59) discovered an increase (compared to what Rosser and Harris had found) to over one-third of their respondents who had lived at their present address for over twenty years, and a similar finding for Luton was reported by Devine (1992: 77) for the mobile workers first studied by Goldthorpe and his colleagues (1969). Pahl was able to contrast this with the 'high level of intra-Island dwelling mobility' (1984: 183) that his survey had discovered. He argued that it reflected a distinctive attitude of Sheppey people towards the use of housing improvement to pursue upward social mobility. It can therefore be intriguing if repeating a research question throws up different findings.

This is not to say that community studies researchers should have responded to the criticism of being like second-rate novel writers by adopting a standardized template. As Brunt has observed, community studies 'remind us time and again of the subjectiveness and onesidedness of social perception' (2001: 84), including that of researchers, and we would expect reports of findings to vary. By having leeway to follow up different things that struck them as interesting and engaging, we have the benefit of Keller mentioning that in the early years of the Twin Rivers development the social events included 'Husband Appreciation Night' (2003: 113), something another researcher might have overlooked. Similarly we have Blokland's perceptiveness to credit for relating the story from her respondent of how in Hillesluis in the first half of the twentieth century the division between Catholics and Protestants was reproduced in tensions about trade union organization, with Protestant workers being stigmatized as 'the EVC, the Eternal Vacation Club, of course that wasn't its real name but we called it that ... they had strikes all the time' (2003: 137). A third example of the potential for community studies to be more poetic than prosaic is Middletown resident Dolores Rhinehart's elaboration in the film that accompanies Lassiter and his colleagues' (2004) book of her point about the need for people on low incomes to manage money carefully: 'Don't drink champagne if you're on a beer budget!'. A variation on this theme is the use by Bill Williamson of his grandfather's expression, 'See to your needs first, then your wants' (1982: v) as a way of introducing him as a Northumberland coal miner from a bygone age with a life story of contemporary relevance.

Such vignettes can be extended. Williamson's book uses the life story of his grandfather James Brown as a means for presenting 'a biographical study of social change in mining', and 'to show that biography is a form of writing and analysis appropriate to the study of social change' (1982: 1). Pahl's account of Linda and Jim towards the end of his book also sets out to follow Mills in linking biography and history. Rosser and Harris did something similar with Mr Griffith Hughes, with whom they started their book. In the course of the latter's story, the point is made that his Welsh-speaking father, migrating from the countryside, 'could hardly speak a word of English when he first came into Swansea round about 1870' (1965: 8–9). Bilingualism was an issue revisited in Charles and her colleagues' restudy, but with the additional angle to it of parallel processes of adjustment to change among the more recently arrived Sylheti-speaking Bangladeshi community (2008: 109). The restudy replicated the original 'as far as possible' (Charles 2012: 438), but was not prevented from exploring issues of race and ethnicity that had arisen since the 1960s. The community studies tradition contains numerous demonstrations of imagination in terms of both purpose and modes of presentation designed to engage readers (Atkinson 1990). It is sufficiently flexible to evolve and capture emergent social phenomena, and also to find new ways of recounting the diverse routes by which we have come to be where we are.

6 Summary and where next?

A short book cannot provide an exhaustive coverage of community studies, but the preceding chapters have sought to make and illustrate five key points about the community studies tradition of research. These are that community studies are bold in their ambition to highlight the connectedness of social and economic life through analyses that place this connectedness in context; that an evolving range of methodological tools are available to pursue this goal; that community studies' findings have the potential to be both of practical use and theoretically interesting; that this tradition of research has a history that continues to be reworked as the world around us and our tools for understanding it develop; and that community studies give rise to impassioned discussion about what should be studied, and how and why. These things are not unique to community studies, but it is not every branch of social scientific endeavour that records researchers being at one extreme fêted as champions of ordinary people yet at the other being hanged in effigy by unhappy readers.

To begin with the fifth of these points, it has not been possible to resolve to everyone's satisfaction the what, how and why questions. The meaning of 'community' remains contentious, as does the related issue of what constitutes a community study. Despite Warner's expectations that he would, Goffman did not write up his fieldwork on Unst as a community study; he introduced his report by saying, 'This is not the study *of* a community: it is a study that occurred, *in* a community' (1953: 8, emphases in original). So community studies are a subset of research undertaken on communities. The examples of community studies considered in this book vary in the ways that they go about exploring the connectedness of different parts of everyday social and economic life, but these are variations on the theme first articulated by the Lynds that people's work, home, school, leisure, religious and political lives are intertwined, underpinned by the related (Durkheimian) observation that the whole is greater than the sum of the parts. These patterns of connection are often, but do not have to be, place related. The precise relationship of community to place continues to be debated in the wake of the demise of attempts to link them deterministically (Cresswell 2004), a discussion to which several studies examined above have contributed. Blokland's observation that 'everybody has to live somewhere' is one example, and her book's maps help to convey the point. She also uses her findings to contest Wellman's reduction of 'community' to personal networks because this fails to include the '"imagined" aspect of communities' (2003: 158, 24, 29, 60). Different conceptualizations of 'community' thus connect to different operationalizations of the concept in empirical research (Crow and Mah 2012). There are also different rationales offered for undertaking community studies, both practical and theoretical, as discussed in Chapter 4.

Rationales matter, because community studies are not undertaken lightly. Most of the community studies referred to in the chapters above have been books, a format that allows fuller exposition than journal articles. They typically take years to complete, even decades, through either the employment of a team or the efforts of the generalist researcher captured in Bell's description of 'the sociological jack-of-all-trades that doing a community study requires' (1977: 61). As Glass noted, the purpose of a community study is 'to show a "total" picture' (1989: 87), and the original Middletown study that she commended ran to 550 pages. Even the shortest of the six topics considered in the book (training the young) had over forty pages devoted to it and this alone exceeded the size of a typical article, while the length of the longest of the six (engaging in religious practices) was more than double this length (Lynd and Lynd 1929). Ironically this topic, which had provided the springboard for the study, is one that subsequent researchers have been prepared to drop as part of efforts to make undertaking a community study manageable (discussion of religion is missing from *Divisions of Labour* and *The British on the Costa del Sol*, for example). Community studies are expensive in terms of time, resources and commitment, and the remarkably speedy delivery of *The Other Side of Middletown* was achieved only because of the team's exceptional resourcefulness and commitment.

The Lynds' ambitious agenda may have been pared down in many subsequent studies by dropping one or more of their six topics in order to achieve a feasible focus on a more manageable pattern of connection. Even if we leave to one side the demands to speed up that characterize 'the age of accelerations' (Friedman 2016), there are several reasons why the classical

community study format has come under pressure. Methodological innovations and concern to highlight the importance of social and economic
phenomena being placed in context have encouraged more comparative
work, through comparisons between places (as was noted in Chapter 5's
discussion of responses to the charge of parochialism), or through comparison over time (facilitated, for example, through the developments in
oral history and use of archival material). There are also new things that
researchers have sought to include, such as Corcoran and her colleagues'
(2010) decision to give voice to children in their study of suburbia; as a
result they provide a more authentic account than is typically the case
when children are merely spoken for by adults, or simply left out altogether.
Community studies have a proud tradition of giving voice to social groups
not usually heard, sometimes taking their lead from developments in
neighbouring research fields (in this case childhood studies (Mayall 2002)).

The argument that changes in research practice have been necessary
for men's perspective to be captured is somewhat surprising given that
community studies have been criticized for problematic portrayals of
women, but the case bears scrutiny. Charles and her colleagues report
that 'it was more difficult to find men than women who would agree
to be interviewed' (2008: 43), so that women (who were regarded by
many of the potential participants that they contacted as better placed
to speak about family matters) comprised 63 per cent of their sample.
Pahl achieved greater success in avoiding survey data collected 'dispro-
portionately from either men or women' (1984: 201), possibly reflecting
his research focus on work, but certainly due to innovation in sampling
practice. Phillipson and his colleagues were unsurprised that their sample
of older people was 62 per cent female because of the (then) earlier age of
retirement for women, but they were still concerned about 'the absence of
men' (2001: 31, 9) as expressed in the photographic record of the past and
the written record in classic studies that had focused on matrilocal (and
arguably matriarchal) networks. McKenzie devotes a whole chapter to 'the
missing men' with whom she had crossed paths very little in her previous
research on the St Ann's estate in Nottingham, when she had been guided
by the maxim 'if you want to know anything about a neighbourhood, ask
the women' (2015: ch.3, 52). She reports being able to track down the men
easily enough, once she had appreciated that they spent their time in different places to the women of the estate, such as the gym, and had useful
additional perspectives to add.

McKenzie's research revisits the location of Coates and Silburn's (1973, 1980) studies of poverty and develops the familiar theme of community change and continuity. The old slum housing has gone through wholesale regeneration, but the story is an object lesson of how compound social problems cannot be solved one at a time; the area remains 'a neighbourhood of disadvantage' (2015: 39). The understanding of the community's multiple deprivation is undoubtedly useful, but the way in which the book is written is also interesting theoretically, particularly for the discussion of the misperception of people living on poor estates. There are echoes of William Foote Whyte's classic study *Street Corner Society* in which he describes upper-class ignorance of 'Cornerville', whose residents 'appear as social work clients, as defendants in criminal cases, or as undifferentiated members of "the masses"' (1955: xv). McKenzie draws on Alan Sillitoe's *Saturday Night and Sunday Morning* to make this point about misunderstanding: 'Whatever people say I am, that's what I'm not,' a statement by the novel's central character that conveys the anger generated by misrepresentation and 'being "looked down on"' by people on the outside. Her concluding comment lamenting the 'lack of positive namings' (2015: 25, 76, 201) of communities like St Ann's says something not only about familiar processes of stigmatization, but also about the challenge of how communities get defined. This is not unique to disadvantaged communities but more general. O'Reilly's remark that 'it is easier to describe Britons in Spain in terms of what they are not than what they are' is made in the context of discussing how, despite their many differences, they could all contrast their situation with what they had left behind; life in Spain was understood in terms of 'all the opposites of what Britain is, namely crime, greyness, drudgery, routine, certainty, scripting' (2000a: 157–8), disregarding the fact that their narratives of hope and pursuit of a dream were recognizably scripted. Anya Ahmed's more recent study of women retirees in Spain supports this idea that they had been taken there by a shared quest to live among 'people like us' (2015: 126). Immigration into Britain had in their view made living there problematic. A positive image of one's own community is reinforced by a negative one of another (Cohen 1985), and the images become reinforced when a restricted range of social contact leaves people 'insulated' (Newby et al. 1978: 209) from alternative points of view.

This issue of how understandings of 'community' are constructed is made particularly interesting by fundamental ways in which the world is changing. Martin Albrow's observation that 'the moment migration enters into the frame for community studies a new range of questions arises' (1997: 41) highlights a key challenge concerning the very categories of community members. It is worth remembering that the Banbury restudy spoke of more than half of the people living in the town being 'immigrants' (Stacey et al. 1975: 13), defining these as people not born in Banbury, harking back to an earlier era when people were less mobile. Over time the insider/outsider distinction came under increasing strain, and Savage and his colleagues use the finding that 'insiders and outsiders do not exist as fixed categories' to argue that length of residence has become less important to community membership than 'elective belonging', described as a new kind of solidarity 'among people who chose to live in particular places' (2005: 31, 53). This fits with the string of findings covered in the preceding chapters in which community is understood as being among 'people like us', as when Blokland refers to the process of imagining communities constructed out of like-minded people and with an external reference group. In this thinking 'we belong together; they belong together, and they do not belong with us' (2003: 63). In an age of frequent mobility, including mobility on an international scale such as that described by Levitt (2001) and O'Reilly (2000a), previously used distinctions such as that between insiders and outsiders require fundamental reconsideration, along with more systematic empirical investigation of whether 'elective belonging' applies as much to tenants as it appears to apply to owner-occupiers. It follows that research methods will need to change along with analytical frameworks if the tradition of research being useful and interesting is to be sustained.

Diversity of theoretical and methodological approaches is a key characteristic of the community studies tradition. This openness to a plurality of approaches has periodically been the subject of critical assessment, but the stance adopted here is that it offers the flexibility and openness to innovation that are important for sustainability into the future. The case for pluralism was set out by Colin Bell and Howard Newby, informed among other things by their (Bell and Encel 1978; Bell and Newby 1971, 1974; Newby et al. 1978; Stacey et al. 1975) knowledge of community studies, which fed into their view that there cannot 'be only one style of social research with *one* method that is to be *the* method. Rather there are many' (1977: 10, emphases in original). Developments in social science in the ensuing period have seen the range of methods available (either singly or in combination) continue to grow, and *Divisions of Labour* was selected as one of the exemplars in Chapter 3 because of its ambitiousness in combining multiple methods. Mixing methods may now be the norm in community research, if the one hundred items considered in a recent annotated bibliography are a guide, since most of these used a combination of two or more methods, including interviews, ethnography (or participant observation), case studies, policy analyses, surveys, discourse, media or textual analyses, visual methods, archival methods, participatory methods, focus groups, network analyses, online/virtual methods and mobile methods (Mah and Crow 2011: 1). Current practice has moved a long way from the 'imperialism' that Bell and Newby (1977: 17) warned against, although tolerance of pluralism is not universal. Lassiter indicates that there are 'those who dismiss collaborative research outright' and others who believe that it is 'always appropriate for all types of research' (2005: xi), to give one example of a field where 'methodolatry' (Bell and Newby 1977: 16) can still be found.

Theoretical and methodological pluralism do not mean that decisions about analytical frames and tools of investigation are inconsequential. These choices matter, both for the quality of the resultant research, and also for the researcher. The outputs of community studies reveal something about the researcher as well as the topic under investigation, and it remains true that 'the great studies ... always have the quality of individuality, integrity and discovery' (Vidich and Bensman 1971: vii). The discussion in Chapter 3 of the exemplars was sufficiently extensive to convey something about their authors' qualities and the learning curves on which they found themselves. The researcher's investment of him or herself in the research process is an important reason why restudies can never be simple replications, because no two researchers will approach things in identical ways. McKenzie's (2015) return to St Ann's as someone with decades of first-hand experience of living there gives her account a very different colour to those of Coates and Silburn (1973, 1980), notwithstanding the similarities of their motivations as researchers. The issues raised by community research being done by 'insiders' as opposed to 'outsiders' will continue to be the subject of intense debate (not least because these terms are contested by some people as insufficiently nuanced), along with the discussion of the relative merits of individual and team approaches. *The Other Side of Middletown* demonstrates that teams can not only involve both insiders and outsiders, but also incorporate ways of working collaboratively and creatively. The intensification of time pressures on researchers, including demands to produce results quickly, suggests that research students will continue to generate a significant proportion of book-length studies that require the focused commitment of years; *The British on the Costa del Sol* has been our exemplar. And the growing availability of material archived by researchers at the end of their projects allows more modest partial restudies to be undertaken. Dawn Lyon's (2017) revisiting of Sheppey with colleagues could not hope to match the scale of *Divisions of Labour*, but nevertheless adds to knowledge of that community. Such developments are very much in the spirit of pluralism which has characterized the community studies tradition and which promises to underpin its continued vitality.

References

Abrams, P. (1978). 'Introduction: Social facts and sociological analysis'. In P. Abrams (ed.), *Work, Urbanism and Inequality: U.K. Society Today* London: Weidenfeld and Nicolson, pp. 1–16.

Abrams, P. and McCulloch, A. (1976). *Communes, Sociology and Society* Cambridge: Cambridge University Press.

Ahmed, A. (2015). *Retiring to Spain: Women's Narratives of Nostalgia, Belonging and Community* Bristol: Policy Press.

Albrow, M. (1997). 'Travelling beyond local cultures: socioscapes in a global city'. In J. Eade (ed.), *Living the Global City: Globalization as Local Process* London: Routledge, pp. 37–55.

Allan, G. (1979). *A Sociology of Friendship and Kinship* London: George Allen and Unwin.

Amit, V. (2002). 'Reconceptualizing community'. In V. Amit (ed.), *Realizing Community: Concepts, Social Relationships and Sentiments* London: Routledge, pp. 1–20.

Anderson, B. (1991). *Imagined Communities: Reflections on the Origin and Spread of Nationalism*. London: Verso, second edition.

Anwar, M. (1985). *The Myth of Return* London: New Century.

Atkinson, P. (1990). *The Ethnographic Imagination: Textual Constructions of Reality* London: Routledge.

Bauman, Z. (2001). *Community* Cambridge: Polity.

Baumann, G. (1996). *Contesting Culture: Discourses of Identity in Multi-Ethnic London* Cambridge: Cambridge University Press.

Baumgartner, M. (1988). *The Moral Order of a Suburb* New York: Oxford University Press.

Bell, C. (1977). 'Reflections on the Banbury restudy'. In C. Bell and H. Newby (eds), *Doing Sociological Research* London: George Allen and Unwin, pp. 47–62.

Bell, C. and Encel, S. (eds) (1978) *Inside the Whale: Ten Personal Accounts of Social Research* Rushcutters Bay NSW: Pergamon Press.

Bell, C. and Newby, H. (1971). *Community Studies* London: George Allen and Unwin.

Bell, C. and Newby, H. (eds) (1974). *The Sociology of Community* London: Frank Cass.

Bell, C. and Newby, H. (1977). 'Introduction: The Rise of Methodological Pluralism'. In C. Bell and H. Newby (eds), *Doing Sociological Research* London: George Allen and Unwin, pp. 9–29.

Bell, M. (1994). *Childerley: Nature and Morality in a Country Village* Chicago: University of Chicago Press.

Benson, M. (2011). *The British in Rural France. Lifestyle Migration and the Ongoing Quest for a Better Way of Life* Manchester: Manchester University Press.

Berger, B. (1968). *Working-Class Suburb: A Study of Auto Workers in Suburbia* Berkeley: University of California Press.

Blackshaw, T. (2010). *Community Studies* London: Sage.

Blokland, T. (2003). *Urban Bonds: Social Relationships in an Inner City Neighbourhood* Cambridge: Polity.

Blokland, T. and Noordhoff, F. (2008). 'The weakness of weak ties: Social capital to get ahead among the urban poor in Rotterdam and Amsterdam'. In T. Blokland and M. Savage (eds), *Networked Urbanism* Farnham: Ashgate, pp. 105–25.

Brent, J. (2009). *Searching for Community* Bristol: Policy Press.

Briggs, A. (2001). *Michael Young: Social Entrepreneur* Basingstoke: Palgrave.

Brody, H. (1973). *Inishkillane: Change and Decline in the West of Ireland* London: Allen Lane.

Brook, E. and Finn, D. (1978). 'Working class images of society and community studies'. In Centre for Contemporary Cultural Studies, *On Ideology* London: Hutchinson, pp. 125–43.

Brunt, L. (2001). 'Into the community'. In P. Atkinson, A. Coffey, S. Delamont, J. Lofland and L. Lofland (eds), *Handbook of Ethnography* London: Sage, pp. 80–91.

Bryson, A. and McKay, S., eds (1994). *Is It Worth Working? Factors Affecting Labour Supply* London: Policy Studies Institute.

Bryson, L. and Thompson, F. (1972). *An Australian Newtown* Harmondsworth: Penguin.

Bryson, L. and Winter, I. (1999). *Social Change, Suburban Lives: An Australian Newtown 1960s to 1990s*. St Leonards, NSW: Allen and Unwin.

Bulmer, M. (1984). *The Chicago School of Sociology* Chicago: University of Chicago Press.

Bulmer, M. (1985). 'The rejuvenation of community studies? Neighbours, networks and policy'. *Sociological Review* 33, pp. 430–48.

Bulmer, M. (1986). *Neighbours: The Work of Phillip Abrams* Cambridge: Cambridge University Press.

Burgess, R. (2001). 'Never mind the quality…? Developments in ethnographic qualitative research'. In R. Burgess and A. Murcott (eds), *Developments in Sociology* Harlow: Prentice Hall, pp. 35–49.

Butler, T. with Robson, G. (2003). *London Calling: The Middle Classes and the Re-making of Inner London* Oxford: Berg.

Caccamo, R. (2000). *Back to Middletown: Three Generations of Sociological Reflections* Stanford: Stanford University Press.

Campbell, E. and Lassiter, L. E. (2014). *Doing Ethnography Today: Theories, Methods, Exercises* Chichester: Wiley-Blackwell.

Charles, N. (2012). 'Families, communities and social change: then and now'. *Sociological Review* 60(3), pp. 438–56.

Charles, N., Davies, C. and Harris, C. (2008). *Families in Transition: Social Change, Family Formation and Kin Relationships* Bristol: Policy Press.

Charlesworth, S. (2000). *A Phenomenology of Working Class Experience* Cambridge: Cambridge University Press.

Coates, K. and Silburn, R. (1973). *Poverty: The Forgotten Englishmen* Harmondsworth: Penguin.

Coates, K. and Silburn, R. (1980). *Beyond the Bulldozer* Nottingham: University of Nottingham.

Cohen, A., ed. (1982). *Belonging: Identity and Social Organisation in British Rural Cultures* Manchester: Manchester University Press.

Cohen, A. (1985). *The Symbolic Construction of Community* London: Routledge.

Cohen, A., ed. (1986). *Symbolising Boundaries: Identity and Diversity in British Cultures* Manchester: Manchester University Press.

Cohen, A. (1987). *Whalsay: Symbol, Segment and Boundary in a Shetland Island Community* Manchester: Manchester University Press.

Corcoran, M., Gray, J. and Peillon, M. (2010). *Suburban Affiliations: Social Relations in the Greater Dublin Area* Syracuse: Syracuse University Press.

Cornwell, J. (1984). *Hard-Earned Lives* London: Tavistock.

Cresswell, T. (2004). *Place: A Short Introduction* Oxford: Blackwell.

Crow. G. (1989). 'The use of the concept of "strategy" in recent sociological literature'. *Sociology* 23(1), pp. 1–24.

Crow, G. (2000). 'Developing sociological arguments through community studies'. *International Journal of Social Research Methodology* 3(3), pp. 173–87.

Crow, G. (2002a). *Social Solidarities* Buckingham: Open University Press.

Crow, G. (2002b). 'Community studies: Fifty years of theorization'. *Sociological Research On-line* 7(3), http://www.socresonline.org.uk/socresonline/7/3

Crow, G. (2005). *The Art of Sociological Argument* Basingstoke: Palgrave Macmillan.

Crow, G. (2012). 'Community re-studies: Lessons and prospects'. *Sociological Review* 60(3), pp. 405–20.

Crow, G. (2013). 'Going back to re-study communities: Challenges and opportunities'. *Progress in Development Studies* 13(4), pp. 267–78.

Crow, G. (2014). 'The sociology of community'. In J. Holmwood and J. Scott (eds), *The Palgrave Handbook of Sociology in Britain* Basingstoke: Palgrave Macmillan, pp. 374–95.

Crow, G. and Allan, G. (1994). *Community Life* Hemel Hempstead: Harvester Wheatsheaf.

Crow, G., Allan, G. and Summers, M. (2002). 'Neither Busybodies nor nobodies: Managing proximity and distance in neighbourly relations'. *Sociology* 36(1), pp. 127–45.

Crow, G. and Ellis, J. (eds) (2017). *Revisiting Divisions of Labour* Manchester: Manchester University Press.

Crow, G. and Maclean, C. (2013). 'Community'. In G. Payne (ed.), *Social Divisions*, 3rd edn. Basingstoke: Palgrave Macmillan, pp. 352–71.

Crow, G. and Mah, A. (2012). Conceptualisations and meanings of 'community': The theory and operationalisation of a contested concept, http://www.community-methods.soton.ac.uk/index.php

Crow, G. and Pope, C. (2008). 'Editorial foreword: The future of the research relationship'. *Sociology* 42(5), pp. 813–9.

Crow, G. and Takeda, N. (2011). 'Ray Pahl's sociological career: Fifty years of impact', *Sociological Research Online* 16(3), http://www.socresonline.org.uk/16/3/11.html

Davies, C. (1999). *Reflexive Ethnography: A Guide to Researching Selves and Others* London: Routledge.

Day, G. (2006). *Community and Everyday Life* Abingdon: Routledge.

Dempsey, K. (1990). *Smalltown: A Study of Social Inequality, Cohesion and Belonging* Melbourne: Oxford University Press.

Dempsey, K. (1992). *A Man's Town: Inequality Between Women and Men in Rural Australia* Melbourne: Oxford University Press.

Dench, G., Gavron, K. and Young, M. (2006). *The New East End: Kinship, Race and Conflict* London: Profile.

Dennis, N., Henriques, F. and Slaughter, C. (1969). *Coal Is Our Life: An Analysis of a Yorkshire Mining Community* London: Tavistock.

Devine, F. (1992). *Affluent Workers Revisited: Privatism and the Working Class* Edinburgh: Edinburgh University Press.

Eade, J. (1989). *The Politics of Community: The Bangladeshi Community in East London* Aldershot: Avebury.

Eade, J., (ed.) (1997). *Living the Global City: Globalization as Local Process* London: Routledge.

Elias, N. (1974). 'Towards a theory of communities'. In C. Bell and H. Newby (eds), *The Sociology of Community* London: Frank Cass, pp. ix–xli.

Elias, N. (1978). *What is Sociology?* London: Hutchinson.

Elias, N. (1991). *The Society of Individuals* Oxford: Basil Blackwell.

Elias, N. (1994). 'Introduction'. In N. Elias and J. Scotson (eds), *The Established and the Outsiders* London: Sage, second edition, pp. xv–lii.

Elias, N. and Scotson, J. (1994). *The Established and the Outsiders* London: Sage, second edition.

Elliott, J. and Lawrence, J. (2017). 'Narrative, time and intimacy in social research: Linda and Jim revisited'. In G. Crow and J. Ellis (eds), *Revisiting Divisions of Labour* Manchester: Manchester University Press, pp. 189–204.

Eriksen, T. (2001). *Small Places, Large Issues: An Introduction to Social and Cultural Anthropology* London: Pluto Press, second edition.

Farrar, M. (2002). *The Struggle for 'Community' in a British Multi-ethnic Inner-city Area: Paradise in the Making* Lampeter: Edwin Mellen.

Fine, B. (2010). *Theories of Social Capital* London: Pluto Press.

Finnegan, R. (1989). *The Hidden Musicians: Music-making in an English Town* Cambridge: Cambridge University Press.

Foster, J. (1990). *Villains: Crime and Community in the Inner City* London: Routledge.

Foster, J. (1999). *Docklands: Cultures in Conflict, Worlds in Collision* London: UCL Press.

Fox, R. (1978). *The Tory Islanders: A people of the Celtic fringe* Cambridge: Cambridge University Press.

Frankenberg, R. (1969). *Communities in Britain* Harmondsworth: Penguin.

Frankenberg, R. (1976). 'In the production of their lives, men (?) ... sex and gender in British community studies', In D. Leonard Barker and S. Allen (eds), *Sexual Divisions and Society* London: Tavistock, pp. 25–51.

Frankenberg, R. (1990). *Village on the Border* Prospect Heights, IL: Waveland Press.

Friedman, T. (2016). *Thank You For Being Late: An Optimist's Guide to Thriving in the Age of Accelerations* London: Allen Lane.

Gallaher, A. (1961). *Plainville Fifteen Years Later* New York: Columbia University Press.

Gans, H. (1962a). 'Urbanism and Suburbanism as Ways of Life'. In A. Rose (ed.), *Human Behaviour and Social Processes* London: Routledge and Kegan Paul.

Gans, H. (1962b). *The Urban Villagers: Group and Class in the Life of Italian-Americans* New York: Free Press.

Gans, H. (1967). *The Levittowners: Ways of Life and Politics in a New Suburban Community* New York: Vintage.

Gavron, K. and Mulgan, G. (2007). 'Introduction to the 2007 edition'. In M. Young and P. Willmott (eds), *Family and Kinship in East London* Harmondsworth: Penguin, pp. vii–xii.

Giarchi, G. (1984). *Between McAlpine and Polaris* London: Routledge and Kegan Paul.

Glaser, B. and Strauss, A. (1967). *The Discovery of Grounded Theory: Strategies for Qualitative Research* Chicago: Aldine.

Glass, R. (1989). *Clichés of Urban Doom and Other Essays* Oxford: Blackwell.

Goffman, A. (2014). *On The Run: Fugitive Life in an American City* Chicago: Chicago University Press.

Goffman, E. (1953). Communication Conduct In an Island Community. PhD Dissertation, University of Chicago, https://archive.org/details/GOFFMAN1953CommunicationConductInAnIslandCommunity

Goffman, E. (1969). *The Presentation of Self in Everyday Life* Harmondsworth: Penguin.

Goffman, E. (2002). 'On fieldwork'. In D. Weinberg (ed.), *Qualitative Research Methods* Oxford: Blackwell, pp. 148–53.

Goldthorpe, J., Lockwood, D., Bechhofer, F. and Platt, J. (1969). *The Affluent Worker in the Class Structure* Cambridge: Cambridge University Press.

Granovetter, M. (1973). 'The Strength of Weak Ties'. *American Journal of Sociology* 78(6), 1360–80.

Gregory, S. and Hartley, G. (eds) (1991). *Constructing Deafness* London: Frances Pinter.

Gruzd, A., Wellman, B. and Takhteyev, Y. (2011). 'Imagining Twitter as an Imagined community'. *American Behavioural Scientist* 55(10), pp. 1294–1318.

Hall, S. (2012). *City, Street and Citizen: The Measure of the Ordinary* London: Routledge.

Hammersley, M. (2016). 'Reflections on the value of ethnographic re-studies: Learning from the past'. *International Journal of Social Research Methodology* 19(5), pp. 537–50.

Hammersley, M. and Atkinson, P. (2007). *Ethnography: Principles in Practice* Third edition. London: Routledge.

Harper, D. (1982). *Good Company* Chicago: University of Chicago Press.

Harper, D. (1987). *Working Knowledge: Skill and Community in a Small Shop* Berkeley: University of California Press.

Harper, D. (1992). 'Small N's and community case studies'. In C. Ragin and H. Becker (eds), *What Is A Case? Exploring the Foundations of Social Inquiry* Cambridge: Cambridge University Press, pp. 139–58.

Harper, D. (2001), *Changing Works: Visions of a Lost Agriculture* Chicago: University of Chicago Press.

Harris, C. (1987), *Redundancy and Recession* Oxford: Blackwell.

Hochschild, A. (1973), *The Unexpected Community: Portrait of An Old Age Subculture* Berkeley: University of California Press.

Holme, A. (1985), *Housing and Young Families in East London* London: Routledge and Kegan Paul.

Hornsby, A. (2013), 'Surfing the net for community: A Durkheimian analysis of electronic gatherings'. In P. Kivisto (ed.), *Illuminating Social Life: Classical and Contemporary Theory Revisited* London: Sage, pp. 51–94.

Hughes, E. (1971). 'French Canada: The natural history of a research project'. In A. Vidich, J. Bensman and M. Stein (eds), *Reflections on Community Studies* New York: Harper and Row, pp. 71–83.

Hunter, A. (1974). *Symbolic Communities* Chicago: University of Chicago Press.

Hunter, J. (1976). *The Making of the Crofting Community* Edinburgh: John Donald.

Igo, S. (2007). *The Averaged American: Surveys, Citizens, and the Making of a Mass Public* Cambridge, MA: Harvard University Press.

Jackson, A., (ed.) (1987). *Anthropology at Home.* London: Tavistock.

Jahoda, M., Lazarsfeld, P. and Zeisel, H. (1972). *Marienthal: The Sociography of an Unemployed Community* London: Tavistock.

Jamieson, L. and Toynbee, C. (1992). *Country Bairns: Growing Up 1900–1930* Edinburgh: Edinburgh University Press.

Jordan, T. (2002). 'Community, everyday and space'. In T. Bennett and D. Watson (eds), *Understanding Everyday Life* Oxford: Blackwell, pp. 229–69.

Karn, V. (1977). *Retiring to the Seaside* London: Routledge and Kegan Paul.

Keller, S. (2003). *Community: Pursuing the Dream, Living the Reality* Princeton, NJ: Princeton University Press.

Kent, R. (1981). *A History of British Empirical Sociology* Aldershot: Gower.

Kerr, M. (1958). *The People of Ship Street* London: Routledge and Kegan Paul.

King, R., Warnes, T. and Williams, A. (2000). *Sunset Lives: British Retirement Migration to the Mediterranean* Oxford: Berg.

Lassiter, L. E. (2005). *The Chicago Guide to Collaborative Ethnography* Chicago: Chicago University Press.

Lassiter, L. E. (2012). '"To fill the missing piece of the Middletown puzzle": Lessons from re-studying Middletown'. *Sociological Review* 60(3), 421–37.

Lassiter, L. E., Goodall, H., Campbell, E. and Johnson, M. (2004). *The Other Side of Middletown: Exploring Muncie's African American Community* Lanham: AltaMira Press.

Lee, D. and Newby, H. (1983). *The Problem of Sociology* London: Hutchinson.

Levitt, P. (2001). *The Transnational Villagers* Berkeley: University of California Press.

Lewis, O. (1963). *Life in a Mexican Village: Tepoztlán Revisited* Urbana: University of Illinois Press.

Ling, R. (2008). *New Tech, New Ties: How Mobile Communication is Reshaping Social Cohesion* Cambridge, MA: MIT Press.

Littlejohn, J. (1963). *Westrigg: The Sociology of a Cheviot Parish* London: Routledge and Kegan Paul.

Low, S. (2003). *Behind the Gates: Life, Security and the Pursuit of Happiness in Fortress America* New York: Routledge.

Lummis, T. (1985). *Occupation and Society: The East Anglian Fishermen 1880–1914* Cambridge: Cambridge University Press.

Lynd, R. (1939). *Knowledge for What? The Place of Social Science in American Culture* Princeton: Princeton University Press.

Lynd, R. and Lynd, H. (1929). *Middletown: A Study in Contemporary American Culture* New York: Harcourt Brace.

Lynd, R. and Lynd, H. (1937). *Middletown in Transition: A Study in Cultural Conflicts* New York: Harcourt and Brace.

Lyon, D. (2017). 'Time and place in memory and imagination on the Isle of Sheppey'. In G. Crow and J. Ellis (eds), *Revisiting Divisions of Labour.* Manchester: Manchester University Press, pp. 149–68.

Madge, J. (1970). *The Origins of Scientific Sociology* London: Tavistock.

Mah, A. (2012). *Industrial Ruination, Community, and Place: Landscapes and Legacies of Urban Decline* Toronto: University of Toronto Press.

Mah, A. and Crow, G. (2011). Researching Community in the Twenty-first century: An annotated bibliography, http://www.community-methods. soton.ac.uk/index.php

Martin, E. (1965). *The Shearers and the Shorn* London: Routledge and Kegan Paul.

Mayall, B. (2002). *Towards a Sociology for Childhood: Thinking from children's lives* Buckingham: Open University Press.

McDonald, L. (1994). *The Women Founders of the Social Sciences* Ottawa: Carleton University Press.

McKenzie, L. (2015). *Getting By: Estates, Class and Culture in Austerity Britain* Bristol: Policy Press.

Mennell, S. (1992). *Norbert Elias: An Introduction* Oxford: Blackwell.

Mills, C. W. (1959). *The Power Elite* London: Oxford University Press.

Mills C. W. (2000). *The Sociological Imagination* New York: Oxford University Press.

Modan, G. (2007). *Turf Wars: Discourse, Diversity and the Politics of Place* Oxford: Blackwell.

Mooney, G. and Neal, S. (eds) (2009). *Community: Welfare, crime and Society* Maidenhead: Open University Press.

Moore, R. (1982). *The Social Impact of Oil: The case of Peterhead* London: Routledge and Kegan Paul.

Morgan, D. (2005). 'Revisiting "Communities in Britain"'. *Sociological Review* 53(4), pp. 641–57.

Mumford, K. and Power, A. (2003). *East Enders: Family and Community in East London* Bristol: Policy Press.

Nettle, D. (2015). *Tyneside Neighbourhoods: Deprivation, Social Life and Social Behaviour in One British City* Cambridge: Open Books.

Newby, H., Bell, C., Rose, D. and Saunders, P. (1978). *Property, Paternalism and Power: Class and Control in Rural England* London: Hutchinson.

Okely, J. (1983). *The Traveller-Gypsies* Cambridge: Cambridge University Press.

Oliver, C. (2008). *Retirement Migration: Paradoxes of Ageing* London: Routledge.

O'Reilly, K. (2000a). *The British on the Costa del Sol: Transnational Identities and Local Communities* London: Routledge.

O'Reilly, K. (2000b). 'Trading intimacy for liberty: British women on the costa del sol'. In F. Anthias and G. Lazaridis (eds), *Gender and Migration in Southern Europe: Women on the Move* Oxford: Berg, pp 227–48.

O'Reilly, K. (2005). *Ethnographic Methods* Abingdon: Routledge, second edition.

O'Reilly, K. (2012). 'Ethnographic returning, qualitative longitudinal research and the reflexive analysis of social practice'. *Sociological Review* 60(3), pp. 518–36.

Pahl, R. (1965). *Urbs in Rure* London: LSE.

Pahl, R. (2005). 'Are all communities communities in the mind?' *Sociological Review* 53(4), pp. 621–40.

Pahl, R. E. (1968). 'The rural-urban continuum'. In R. Pahl (ed.), *Readings in Urban Sociology* Oxford: Pergamon, pp. 263–97.

Pahl, R. E. (1973). 'Friends and associates'. In P. Barker (ed.), *A Sociological Portrait* Harmondsworth: Penguin, pp. 76–85.

Pahl, R. E. (1978). 'Living without a job: How school leavers see the future'. *New Society* 2 November, pp. 259–62.

Pahl, R. E. (1980). 'Employment, work and the domestic division of labour'. *International Journal of Urban and Regional Studies* 4, pp. 1–19.

Pahl, R. E. (1982). 'Family, community and unemployment'. *New Society* 21 January, pp. 91–3.

Pahl, R. E. (1984). *Divisions of Labour* Oxford: Basil Blackwell.

Pahl, R. E. and Wallace, C. D. (1988). 'Neither angels in marble nor rebels in red: privatization and working-class consciousness'. In D. Rose (ed.), *Social Stratification and Economic Change* London: Hutchinson, pp. 127–49.

Pappas, G. (1989). *The Magic City: Unemployment in a Working-Class Community* Ithaca: Cornell University Press.

Park, R. (1952). *Human Communities: The city and human ecology* Glencoe, IL: Free Press.

Payne, G. (1996). 'Imagining the community: Some reflections on the community study as a method'. In E. S. Lyon and J. Busfield (eds), *Methodological Imaginations* Basingstoke: Macmillan, pp. 17–33.

Payne, G. and Payne, J. (2004). *Key Concepts in Social Research* London: Sage.

Phillipson, C., Bernard, M., Phillips, J. and Ogg, J. (2001). *The Family and Community Life of Older People: Social Networks and Social Support in Three Urban Areas* London: Routledge.

Pink, S. (2009). *Doing Sensory Ethnography* London: Sage.

Platt, J. (1971). *Social Research in Bethnal Green* London: Macmillan.

Platt, J. (1996). *A History of Sociological Research Methods in America 1920–1960* Cambridge: Cambridge University Press.

Pole, C. and Hillyard, S. (2016). *Doing Fieldwork* London: Sage.

Poplin, D. (1979). *Communities: A Survey of Theories and Methods of Research* New York: Macmillan.

Porter, M. (1993). *Place and Persistence in the Lives of Newfoundland Women* Aldershot: Avebury.

Pryce, K. (1979). *Endless Pressure* Harmondsworth: Penguin.

Putnam, R. (2000). *Bowling Alone: The Collapse and Revival of American Community* New York: Simon and Schuster.

Rapport, N. (1993). *Diverse World-Views in an English Village* Edinburgh: Edinburgh University Press.

Rayside, D. (1991). *A Small Town in Modern Times: Alexandria, Ontario* Montreal: McGill-Queens University Press.

Rees, A. (1951). *Life in a Welsh Countryside* Cardiff: University of Wales Press.

Rex, J. and Moore, R. (1967). *Race, Community and Conflict* Oxford: Oxford University Press.

Richards, L. (1990). *Nobody's Home: Dreams and Realities in a New Suburb* Melbourne: Oxford University Press.

Roberts, I. (1993). *Craft, Class and Control: The Sociology of a Shipbuilding Community* Edinburgh: Edinburgh University Press.

Rogaly, B. and Taylor, B. (2011). *Moving Histories of Class and Community: Identity, Place and belonging in Contemporary England* Basingstoke: Palgrave.

Rosenlund, L. (2009). *Exploring the City with Bourdieu.* Saarbrücken: VDM Verlag Dr Müller.

Rosser, C. and Harris, C. (1965). *The Family and Social Change* London: Routledge and Kegan Paul.

St Leger, F. and Gillespie, N. (1991). *Informal Welfare in Belfast: Caring Communities?* Aldershot: Avebury.

Salaman, G. (1974). *Community and Occupation* Cambridge: Cambridge University Press.

Savage, M. (2010). *Identities and Social Change in Britain since 1940* Oxford: Oxford University Press.

Savage, M., Bagnall, G. and Longhurst, B. (2005). *Globalization and Belonging* London: Sage.

Savage, M. and Warde, A. (1993). *Urban Sociology, Capitalism and Modernity* Basingstoke: Macmillan.

Scheper-Hughes, N. (2001). *Saints, Scholars and Schizophrenics: Mental Illness in Rural Ireland* Berkeley: University of California Press.

Scott, J. (2012). *What Is Social Network Analysis?* London: Bloomsbury Academic.

Scott, J. and Bromley, R. (2013). *Envisioning Sociology* New York: State University of New York Press.

Seeley, J. R., Sim, R. A. and Loosley, E. W. (1963). *Crestwood Heights* New York: John Wiley and Sons.

Shaw, A. (1988). *A Pakistani Community in Britain* Oxford: Blackwell.

Smith, D. M. (1988). *The Chicago School* Basingstoke: Macmillan.

Smith, D. M. (2005). *On the Margins of Inclusion: Changing Labour Markets and Social Exclusion in London* Bristol: Policy Press.

Sparks, R., Girling, E. and Loader, I. (1999). *Crime and Social Change in Middle England: Questions of Order in an English Town* London: Routledge.

Spencer, L. and Pahl, R. (2006). *Rethinking Friendship: Hidden Solidarities Today* Princeton, NJ: Princeton University Press.

Stacey, M. (1960). *Tradition and Change* Oxford: Oxford University Press.

Stacey, M. (1969). 'The myth of community studies'. *British Journal of Sociology* XX, pp. 134–47.

Stacey, M., Batstone, E., Bell, C. and Murcott, A. (1975). *Power, Persistence and Change* London: Routledge and Kegan Paul.

Stein, M. (1964). *The Eclipse of Community* New York: Harper and Row.

Suttles, G. (1968). *The Social Order of the Slum: Ethnicity and Territory in the Inner City* Chicago: Chicago University Press.

Suttles, G. (1972). *The Social Construction of Communities* Chicago: University of Chicago Press.

Thomas, W. and Znaniecki, F. (1927). *The Polish Peasant in Europe and America* New York: Knopf.

Thompson, P, with T. Wailey and T. Lummis (1983). *Living the Fishing* London: Routledge and Kegan Paul.

Thorns, D. (1976). *The Quest for Community: Social Aspects of Residential Growth* London: George Allen and Unwin.

Tunstall, J. (1969). *The Fishermen: The Sociology of an Extreme Occupation* London: MacGibbon and Kee.

Vidich, A. and Bensman, J. (1971). 'The Springdale case: Academic Bureaucrats and sensitive townspeople'. In A. Vidich et al. (eds), *Reflections on Community Studies* New York: Harper and Row, pp. 313–49.

Vidich, A. and Bensman, J. (2000). *Small Town in Mass Society: Class, Power and Religion in a Rural Community* Urbana: University of Illinois Press.

Vidich, A., Bensman, J. and Stein, M., eds (1971). *Reflections on Community Studies* New York: Harper and Row.

Waddington, D., Wykes, M. and Critcher, C. (1991). *Split at the Seams? Community, Continuity and Change after the 1984–5 Coal Dispute* Buckingham: Open University Press.

Wallace, C. (1987). *For Richer, For Poorer: Growing Up In and Out of Work* London: Tavistock.

Warner, W. L. and Lunt, P. (1941). *The Social Life of a Modern Community*, vol. 1, New Haven: Yale University Press.

Warwick, D. and Littlejohn, G. (1992). *Coal, Capital and Culture: A Sociological Analysis of Mining Communities in West Yorkshire* London: Routledge.

Weber, Marianne (1988). *Max Weber: A Biography* New Brunswick: Transaction Books.

Weeks, J., Heaphy, B. and Donovan, C. (2001). *Same Sex Intimacies: Families of Choice and other Life Experiments* London: Routledge.

Wellman, B. (1979). 'The community question: The intimate networks of East Yorkers'. *American Journal of Sociology* 84, pp. 1201–31.

Wellman, B. (1999a). 'Preface'. In B. Wellman (ed.), *Networks in the Global Village: Life in Contemporary Communities* Boulder: Westview, pp. xi–xxi.

Wellman, B. (1999b). 'The network community: An introduction'. In B. Wellman (ed.), *Networks in the Global Village: Life in Contemporary Communities* Boulder: Westview, pp. 1–47.

Wellman, B. and Gulia, M. (1999). 'Net-surfers don't ride alone: Virtual communities as communities'. in B. Wellman (ed.), *Networks in the Global Village: Life in Contemporary Communities* Boulder: Westview, pp. 331–66.

Wellman, B., Carrington, P. and Hall, A. (1988). 'Networks as personal communities'. In B. Wellman and S. Berkowitz (eds), *Social Structures: A Network Approach* Cambridge: Cambridge University Press, pp. 130–84.

Whyte, W. F. (1955). *Street Corner Society* Chicago: University of Chicago Press.

Wight, D. (1993). *Workers not Wasters: Masculine Respectability, Consumption and Unemployment in Central Scotland* Edinburgh: Edinburgh University Press.

Williams, C. (1981). *Open Cut: The Working Class in an Australian Mining Town* Sydney: George Allen and Unwin.

Williams, G. (1991). *The Welsh in Patagonia: The State and the Ethnic Community* Cardiff: University of Wales Press.

Williams, R. (1975). *The Country and the City*. Frogmore: Paladin.

Williams, R. (1983). *Keywords* London: Fontana.

Williams, W. (1956). *The Sociology of an English Village: Gosforth* London: Routledge and Kegan Paul.

Williamson, B. (1982). *Class, Culture and Community: A Biographical Study of Social Change in Mining* London: Routledge and Kegan Paul.

Willmott, P. (1986). *Social Networks, Informal Care and Public Policy* London: Policy Studies Institute.

Wilson, P. and Pahl, R. E. (1988). 'The changing sociological construct of the family'. *Sociological Review* 36(2), pp. 233–66.

Wirth, L. (1938). 'Urbanism as a way of life'. *American Journal of Sociology* 44(1), pp. 1–24.

Young, M. and Willmott, P. (1957). *Family and Kinship in East London* London: Routledge and Kegan Paul.

Young, M. and Willmott, P. (2006). *Family and Kinship in East London* Harmondsworth: Penguin.

Index